He Turned the World Upside Down

A Fresh Look at the Gospel

Gods Blessing — Lucile —
Robert C Balfour, April, 07 —

R. C. Balfour III

For I am not ashamed of the gospel; it is the power of God for salvation to everyone who has faith…
Rom. 1:16a NRSV

Let anyone who has an ear listen to what the Spirit is saying to the churches. To everyone who conquers, I will give permission to eat from the tree of life that is in the paradise of God. Rev. 2:7 NRSV

Table of Contents

Other books by R. C. Balfour III

In Search of the Aucilla

Fishing for the Abundant Life

Dedication

I dedicate this book to the One Who has inspired every good work I have ever done and Who is responsible for any success I have ever achieved. "...God has highly exalted him and bestowed on him the name which is above every name, that at the name of Jesus every knee should bow, in heaven and on earth and under the earth, and every tongue confess that Jesus Christ is Lord, to the glory of God the Father[1]."

---

[1] Philippians 2: 9-11 RSV.

Acknowledgements

I owe a great debt of thanks to several outstanding clergymen. My own pastor, the Rev. Chuck Bennett has been on standby for the whole period of writing the manuscript. My good friend, the Rev. Bob Slane has helped and given me much encouragement. My friend and illustrator of my first two books, the Rev. Bob Dixon, has offered several important suggestions. The Rev. Cannon Mark A. Pearson has read and re-read the manuscript, offering theological suggestions, Biblical insights, and special punctuation corrections. My wife, Virginia, has copy-read the manuscript and suggested better ways of presenting ideas. Ann King, my first cousin's wife and retired English teacher, has copy-read the manuscript, correcting punctuation and other errors. I would really be remiss if I did not acknowledge the Holy Spirit's role in steering me throughout the manuscript. I just hope I have listened to Him intensely and accurately.

Preface

We are living in a period of trying and difficult conflicts as well as major catastrophes. I cannot make the claim that these are of Biblical proportions or that they signal the beginning of end times. What I can claim is that it is more important than ever for those of us living today to try and understand the Creator, His plan, and our part in it. Have we really assimilated the "Good News" amid all that is going on around us?

The "brave new world of realism" portrayed in the arts and media has brought us very little which is inspiring and almost nothing which is uplifting. It has tempted us and especially the young with a lust for sex, violence, power, and riches. It has made the vulgar acceptable and even edified. The abuse of drugs and alcohol tempts us with experiences reputed to be better than the simple, natural pleasures of life. Many today do not seem to know the *difference* between right and wrong. It is sometimes difficult to find and benefit from the "Good News" in this environment which we have either created or to which we have passively submitted.

This book is a summary of my understanding of Biblical truth—a real contrast to most present day media messages. It comes from many years of trials and blessings and from a great deal of time studying and teaching the Word of God. I hope the message will be helpful to those persevering enough to read it.

I have elected to capitalize the pronouns referring to Jesus Christ. However, the Revised Standard Version and the New Revised Standard Version of the Bible, which I quote often, do not capitalize these pronouns. I hope this inconsistency will not be confusing. I have also taken the liberty to use italics when referring to the major topics of *Messiah*, *Second Coming*, and the *kingdom* of God, as well as in cases where I felt special emphasis should be given. When quoting from the Amplified Bible I could not use italics for emphasis since this version has already italicized certain words. Where I have italicized parts of other Biblical quotations, I have tried to indicate this in the footnotes. The Amplified Bible quotations are written exactly as they appear in that version, with all the parenthesis, brackets, and italics.

Occasionally, my use of the word, "man," is meant to convey "the human race." I use it in the classical, biblical sense—not in any way to convey the sense of gender.

I believe God will richly bless all who earnestly read and digest His Word and are called according to His purpose.

R.C. Balfour III

Part One

Old Covenant and Prophecies

Prologue

There is nothing which will compare with discovering the meaning of life, the essence of the human equation and drama. No amount of riches, power, or fame will compare with it. It is worth more than the wealth of nations and yet is a free gift. It is a profound part of the Creator's purpose but still can be expressed in simple terms. It is more often passed over or thrown aside by "wise men" and intellectuals and revealed instead to the pure in heart.

Modern Man has made great strides in almost every area of science, but his search for meaning has gone almost nowhere. Every once in a while a new approach comes along, gaining in popularity only to stumble back into obscurity. Philosophy, New Age, and liberal Theology have provided little in the way of comfort and direction, leaving much of mankind without a guiding wind or even a rudder. Into such a vacuum it should not be considered unusual when a radical, worldwide movement recruits the young and threatens the entire civilized world order.

Secularism, on the other hand, has been embraced and taught with vigor by many of our institutions of higher learning under the guise of separating the material world we live in from the spiritual. Such thought feeds off political doctrines like the separation of church and state. I believe mistaken interpretations of these doctrines are leading in the wrong direction because they reject the holistic aspect of mankind.[1]

---

[1] Medical science has begun to accept the holistic principle.

Take, for example, the secular approach to creation, which we might call "living in man's time."[2] There is a huge difference between living in man's time and living in God's time.

Man's time began millions of years ago. Somehow, not ever explicitly explained, matter showed up in the void of space. This matter regulated itself into galaxies, stars, planets, suns, etc., all somehow moving in perfect order and harmony. Earth just happened to be located at the exact right distance from its sun, happened to be enclosed in a perfect atmosphere, and happened to be tilted at the perfect angle with ample water on its surface.

Several million years later (with man, great lengths of time explain that which is otherwise irrational) some amorphous protoplasm, deriving from some unknown place in the universe, found its way to earth and worked its way into a single living *cell*. This cell multiplied and became a discernable object of living matter. The process repeated itself many times over a period of several million years until there existed many objects of discernable living matter in the sea and perhaps even on the land. Every million years or so, a discernable piece of living matter mutated into another kind of discernable living matter until a speck of algae appeared in the sea. Eons and multiple mutations later a microscopic shrimp appeared.

I think you get the picture. Another vast gap of mutating time advanced and suddenly there were all sorts of creatures in the sea. There were hundreds of families of different fish, snails, crabs and even mammals. In a certain period of time, which we might call Amorphticene, two of the mammals, one male and one female, jointly decided their kind had had enough of the water. Their progeny developed legs and walked out upon the land. Not content with being stuck on the earth's surface, this creature mutated and developed two wings over another million years,

---

[2] This parody is in no way aimed at legitimate science. Many scientists believe there is no conflict between science and the Creator.

took off and soared into the sky. From there, hundreds of families of birds of all shapes, colors, and sizes mutated and developed.

Some of the land creatures without wings mutated until the jungle, which had also mutated from amorphous protoplasm from an unknown source, was filled with monkeys, apes, chimps, and baboons among hundreds of other types of creatures. We all know it's a relatively small step from there to the development of homo-sapiens, a mutation of perfect order, both male and female with brains which grew larger every million years until we come to modern man and of course modern woman. This creature's amazing brain invented all sorts of creature comforts, but was plagued by the very element which had resulted in its development—man's time. Three score and ten years with a few living slightly longer and each creature died, decayed, and returned to the amorphous protoplasm from which it had grown. *Fini*.

The rest of this book is a narrative of God's time.

I believe that in America and in much of the Western World something of great, even inestimable value has been partially lost. The great pity of it all is that when someone draws our attention to this lost "pearl," there is an immediate outcry from those who have no belief at all. Through the court system and through secular administrators every effort is made to thwart its precious proclamation. I also believe that this "pearl" of greatest value lies partly hidden in the oyster of Judeo-Christian heritage and faith. We have got to be bold enough to shuck away the crusty cover if we are to rediscover the purpose and meaning of life.

It has been my experience that Christianity in its essence, divested of all the trappings and rationalizations hung on it through the years, constitutes a vital Life Force, full of energy, vitality, optimism, healing and hope. I realize that this opinion is contrary to what many intellectuals, secularists and revisionists think,[3] but I believe that giving ourselves over to this Life Force changes us, frees us and saves us. Once experienced, we don't want to walk outside its light again even as we face the busy, modern world, and especially as we face some of life's storms.

Making a decision for Christ liberates us. Our desperate search for meaning is satisfied, our fears and anxieties abated, our misdeeds forgiven, our relations with others improved,   our weaknesses strengthened by the Holy Spirit of God, and our path toward eternity made plain and straight. That's what salvation is all about.

And there's another good thing about it. It doesn't matter who we are— prince or pauper, queen or chamber maid, king of industry or mill hand, we are all counted the same before the Lord. We all have the same invitation to the *kingdom*. Fame and fortune in this world make no difference. Becoming a true child of God is what makes our lives important and what gives them worth.

I believe that the purpose of God and the vitality of the Gospel can be most clearly experienced as we closely examine two extremely important aspects of His plan—the coming of His Anointed One, the *Messiah*, and the coming of His *kingdom*.[4] The

---

[3] The Apostle Paul warns us, "See to it that no one takes you captive through philosophy and empty deceit, according to human traditions, according to the elemental spirits of the universe, and not according to Christ." Colossians 2:8 NRSV.

[4] I have italicized "Messiah" and "kingdom" throughout the book. The only exception is when I quote the Amplified Bible or other versions which do not italicize these words.

drama begins in the Old Testament of the Bible and flows directly through to the New.

One

Beginnings

The story I hope to tell is not about me. It is about One Whom I have encountered many times. His story begins in the Old Testament of the Holy Bible and continues through hundreds of years to the present and far beyond. It is a story which somehow touches every human being who ever lived and reaches all who are to come.

The story begins in the silent, dark void of space. There is absolutely nothing—nothing to be seen—no light or motion just black nothingness. Suddenly a small pin point of light appears. It rapidly grows exponentially and explodes. The enormous blast sends particles of matter off in all directions. As they begin to lose velocity an unseen force (which we call gravity) pulls some together, forming what we now call galaxies. Within the galaxies, the same force collects particles into solar systems, smaller particles rotating around a larger more brilliant mass in the center.

In a few moments of eternity the chaos I have just described stabilizes into a perfectly orchestrated picture of great beauty. Some smaller particles are pulled into the larger masses and explode there. Mimicking the original explosion, an occasional black hole continues to explode, forming new features. The universe has been born and continues to expand.

Being equipped with rational minds, we must ask the question—what produced the light and caused the explosion, creating billions of tons of matter? What force turned chaos into order? What force continued the *directed* path of creation culminating in the formation of a planet with a benign atmosphere, whose surface is three-fourths water? What intelligent force instigated life on earth resulting in myriad families of fish in the sea each one according to its own kind; and birds of the air, each according to its own individual kind, and the beasts of the field—each family different according to its own kind, and plants, grasses, and trees, each one different according to its own kind? What intelligent force brought about all this super-complexity? And last of all, what intelligent force brought about the race of mankind with a brain more complex than the most advanced computer? And what great intelligence blessed humans with memory, reason,[5] skill, creativity and freedom and moved from nothingness to the human personality?

The unseen intellectual presence which produced the universe and the planet earth and life and eventually man, we call God. He is the Creator and the Shaper of human destiny, and He has made His plan and purpose clear in history and in the pages of Holy Scripture.

Just who is *God*? I believe that mankind has too often engaged in sentiment regarding the Creator. For instance, the expression, "God is love"[6] was not meant to *totally* define the Creator. It was meant, in my opinion, to stress one of the Creator's greatest attributes and even used to describe the

---

[5] Based on *The Book of Common Prayer, 1979* p. 370.
[6] 1 John 4:8 b.

relationship God holds with mankind.[7] But to use it as a defining expression of God's *being* is a mistake. God is rather the ultimate cause of all things. A theologian, Paul Tillich, has said that He is the "Ground of Being" or "Being-Itself."[8] Put another way, without Him we have no current, no juice, no life.

The ancient Jew might have come closest to expressing it. He called God "YAHWEH"[9] which means most literally "TO BE." God has within himself the essence of life. He has imparted this essence of life to His Son, Jesus Christ. For any human being to obtain this "life" or be admitted to the *kingdom* of God, Jesus says that a person must be *born again* of water and the Spirit. "That which is born of the flesh is flesh, and that which is born of the Spirit is spirit."[10] John the Baptist said that he baptized with water for the forgiveness of sins, but that One was coming after him Who would baptize with the Holy Spirit.

God obviously does not have a perishable flesh and blood body such as we have. In John 4:24 Jesus tells the Samaritan woman, "God is spirit...." Or, in other words, God has an immortal spiritual body and possesses powers which are too vast for our understanding. If we want to know more about Him, we only have to look at His Son, Jesus Christ, and at the words of Scripture.

---

[7] "The King of love my Shepherd is, whose goodness faileth never; I nothing lack if I am His, and He is mine forever. Perverse and foolish, oft I strayed, But yet in love He sought me, And on his shoulder gently laid, And home rejoicing brought me." 1st and 3rd verses of a hymn written by Henry Williams Baker (1821-1877).

[8] Columbia Encyclopedia Sixth Edition 2001-05, Tillich, Paul Johannes, 1886-1965.

[9] The written Hebrew language did not use vowels so that the name appeared YHWH. In Exodus the name appears as the imperfect tense of the verb, *to be*, the implication being that God exists and can never cease to exist. Also In Exodus when Moses asked God his name, He replied, "Say this to the people of Israel, '*I am* has sent me to you.'"

[10] John 3:6 RSV.

In the book of the prophet Isaiah, we read, "Thus says God the Lord—He Who created the heavens and stretched them forth, He Who spread abroad the earth and that which comes out of it, He Who gives breath to the people on it and spirit to those who walk in it…"[11]

And also in Isaiah: "And therefore the Lord [earnestly] waits [expecting, looking, and longing] to be gracious to you; and therefore He lifts Himself up, that He may have mercy on you and show loving-kindness to you. For the Lord is a God of justice. Blessed (happy, fortunate, to be envied) are all those who [earnestly] wait for Him, who expect and look and long for Him [for His victory, His favor, His love, His peace, His joy, and His matchless, unbroken companionship]!"[12]

Some smart people try to tell us that a million years ago certain things were happening on the earth. They then point out that ten million years ago other events were taking place. I never had much confidence that modern science could tell us such things with any certainty. The phrase from Job comes back to mind, " Where were you when I laid the foundation of the earth? Declare to Me, if you have and know understanding." [13]

The Genesis story tells us a lot about God, creation, and mankind. I have never questioned the *truth* which it pronounces concerning God and man. For instance, "In the beginning God created the heavens and the earth."[14] And God said, "Let us[15] make humankind in our image, according to our likeness; and let them have dominion over the fish of the sea, and over the birds of

---

[11] Isa. 42:5 AB.
[12] Isa. 30: 18 AB.
[13] Job 38:4 AB.
[14] Genesis 1:1 NASB.
[15] Pronouns referring to God, Father and Son, are not capitalized in the RSV or NRSV. In all other instances I have capitalized these pronouns.

the air, and over the cattle, and over the wild animals of the earth, and over every creeping thing that creeps upon the earth."[16] To me these statements are irrefutable. It doesn't matter whether you subscribe to the Big Bang theory, the evolution theory, or some other scientific method. God was primary and He directed the whole affair in accordance with His purpose, regardless of which "creation" theory we believe.

But at this point, the plot thickens. Mankind was in a perfect environment. God supplied all needs. There was no hard labor. There was no malfunction of nature. There was no sickness and there was no death. God spoke directly to mankind. There was no barrier between them. The "Garden" was an ideal place in which to live.

In order to make a creature in His own image, God had blessed mankind with memory, reason, skill,[17] and creativity. The one further attribute He gave mankind was freedom or freewill or the right to make choices entirely independent of God. It was a critical decision, but I believe it had to be done to enable mankind to be more fully "in His image", more fully capable to communicate and react with God.

What followed was an event which shaped the course of mankind for ages to come. A choice was made in direct disobedience to God. Adam (man) was enticed by Eve, his wife, and the serpent (spirit of evil or Satan) to eat fruit of the tree of the knowledge of good and evil. God had set this one limit on our intellectual skills and development. Only He could know what is good and what is evil. He had given ample and sufficient warning against this trespass, even the warning of death,[18] but

---

[16] Genesis 1:26 NRSV.
[17] Based on the *Book of Common Prayer, 1979* p. 370.
[18] Genesis 2:16,17.

Satan lied to Adam and Eve and assured them that they would not die, but would be like God.

Much has been written over the centuries about this unfortunate choice, but we know from the Biblical account that mankind was thrown out of the Garden[19] and thrust into a dangerous environment, where nature was uncontrolled, and aging, sickness and death plagued the human race.[20]   Also mankind had to labor hard for a living. I believe that God did this so that man would realize his dependence on God, and would seek His way and direction. Some would find this way and once again be in communion with the Creator, enjoying the peace and confidence so much needed. Others would not, engulfed in their own pride and conceit.

I have two further observations about the Genesis story. I don't believe God has given up on the "Garden." I believe His purpose is that those who *freely* make the right choices and accept Him and His values eventually will enter His Garden, now called the *kingdom* of *God*. I also believe that man, in his fallen state, has acquired the propensity to create his own concepts of good and evil, casting aside the eternal wisdom of the Creator for that which seems expedient and relative to every situation.

One well known national figure recently was quoted as saying the Ten Commandants are obsolete. He even implied that he could do a better job of writing them. So here we are. No wonder the struggle for meaning is difficult for so many. Our obvious need is for a Savior, Who can reconcile us to our Creator, for One Who can love us so dearly that our hearts are constrained to follow Him and in so doing return to the Garden, the *kingdom* of *God*.

---

[19] Genesis 3:22-24. God had never restricted the tree of *life*. Now, the garden with the tree of life was closed to mankind.
[20] Genesis 3:17-19.

An understanding of the "paradise lost—paradise regained" principle helps many people better understand one of the mysteries of Christianity: why do bad things happen to good people?

Such questions are indeed human but result from a failure to accept the Biblical truth that God had no choice but to evict mankind from the *perfect paradise* of the Garden. Otherwise, a whole race and population of immortal but largely immoral human beings most likely would have resulted. Accordingly, unredeemed mankind was placed in an unredeemed world where the forces of nature are uncontrolled and all things are subject to decay, disease, and death.[21] No one is guaranteed life in this world tomorrow or next week. It can be a fatal mistake to believe that there is plenty of time for repentance. There is no assured time except *now*!

The only corridor back to the Garden is through God himself. In other words man either acknowledges his dependence upon God and accepts His values and His grace or faces uncertain and undesirable consequences. Or as St. Paul put it, "...for the creation was subjected to futility, not of its own will but by the will of him who subjected it in *hope*; because the *creation itself will be set free from its bondage to decay* and obtain the glorious liberty of the children of God. We know that the whole creation has been groaning in travail together until now *(that Christ has appeared)*; and not only the creation, but we ourselves, who have the first fruits of the Spirit, groan inwardly as we wait for the adoption as sons, the redemption of our bodies. For in this *hope* we were saved."[22]

---

[21] Based on Genesis 3:16-19, 22-24.

[22] Rom. 8:20- 24a RSV (my italics and my parenthesis).

Man looks at life from his own short-lived point of view. God looks at eternity. What is best for us for eternity is not easily perceived.[23] That's why some of the principles Jesus taught were misunderstood and even rejected.

Jesus said to His disciples, "If any man would come after me, let him deny himself and take up his cross and follow me. For whoever would save his life will lose it, and whoever loses his life for my sake will find it."[24] A missionary martyred in the jungles of Ecuador a few decades ago illustrates this principle quite well. The following quote was later found in the missionary's diary: "A man is no fool to give up that which he cannot keep, to gain that which he cannot lose."[25]

With eternity in mind, we can surely better believe what St. Paul proclaimed to the Romans, "We know that in everything God works for good with those who love him, who are called according to his purpose."[26]

God of all power, Ruler of the Universe, you are worthy of glory and praise.

Glory to you for ever and ever.

---

[23] Even Peter fell into this trap. When Jesus prophesied that He would be handed over to the Chief Priests and scribes and condemned to death, be killed and rise after three days, Peter took Jesus aside and began to rebuke Him. But Jesus rebuked Peter by saying, "Get thee behind me, Satan! *For you are setting your mind not on divine things but on human things.*" Mark 8:31-33 RSV (my italics).

[24] Matt. 16: 24, 25 RSV.

[25] Excerpt from a sermon by the Rev. Robert Slane. Quoted from a book, "The Shadow of the Almighty" by Elizabeth Elliot, a biography of her martyred husband, Jim Elliot. A primitive tribe murdered the missionaries out of fear of the men exiting from an airplane, which they had never seen. They were later converted to Christ.

[26] Rom.8: 28 RSV.

At your command all things came to be; the vast expanse of interstellar space, galaxies, suns, the planets in their courses, and this fragile earth, our island home.

By your will they were created and have their being.

From the primal elements you brought forth the human race, and blessed us with memory, reason, and skill. You made us the rulers of creation. But we turned against you, and betrayed your trust; and we turned against one another.

Have mercy, Lord, for we are sinners in your sight.[27]

----

1. How do you define God's *being*?
2. What are the basic truths in the Genesis story?
3. Which creation theory do you believe in and how does it relate to the Creator?
4. What decision by mankind led to the Fall? Explain.
5. Why does God allow "bad" things to happen to good people?
6. How can modern man find the way back to the Garden or to the kingdom of God?

Recommended reading: Genesis: Chapter 1
Genesis: 2:15-17
Genesis 3:16-24
Romans: 8:18-25
Acts 17:22-31

---

[27] *The Book of Common Prayer, 1979* p.370.

Two

God Speaks

Following the expulsion from the Garden, mankind was now living in a hazardous environment, but it's not as if God had left the human race to go it alone. He spoke to Noah, a moral and God-fearing man living in the midst of a corrupt civilization. God's instructions were to build a large ark and seek out two, male and female, of every creature on earth. Noah, his family, and the animals were to enter the ark and wait on God. After all this was accomplished, God caused such rain to fall that all living things on earth were destroyed. When the waters receded, God made a covenant with Noah, never again to cause such a flood.

Later, after Noah's linage began to replenish the earth, God spoke to one family of mankind headed by the patriarch, Abraham.[28] God told Abraham to leave his pagan country and set out for a destination which would be shown to him. This destination was not the Garden, but was the first step in closing the divide.

---

[28] Abraham's initial name was Abram, but God changed his name to Abraham, here meaning *father of many nations*.

Abraham, like most other Bible figures, was far from perfect, but he exhibited one outstanding characteristic—*he believed God and for that reason God accepted him as righteous.* God formed an agreement or Covenant with Abraham and his descendents. As long as they followed His commandments and direction, they would be blessed and set aside as a special nation of God's priests and witnesses, free from any stain or influence of paganism.

Passing through foreign lands, Abraham had to accommodate many kings and fight against some. In fear of some rulers, Abraham passed his beautiful wife, Sarah (originally called Sarai), off as his sister.[29] This wily tactic backfired on him and almost got him into trouble, but God was with him and each time he came away with even more wealth and possessions. He finally settled in the land of Canaan, where God had directed him.

God had also promised Abraham that he would be the father of many nations and that his seed would bless many nations. With all his good fortune, Abraham had one serious problem. He had no heir, no son. Sarah had borne him no children. In an effort to solve this problem, Sarah brought her slave girl, Hagar, in to Abraham, urging him to have a child by her. This was indeed accomplished, but being an unholy venture, had unhappy results. A son, Ishmael, was born. This deed was not in accord with God's will and the "new family" soon came into strife with Sarah.

After both Abraham and Sarah were long past the age of conceiving children, the promise of a true son looked hopeless, but God's promise was not to be denied. Sarah conceived and bore Abraham a son, Isaac. To avoid trouble in the family, Hagar and Ishmael were sent out of Abraham's camp. Many think this was the beginning of the Arab-Israeli conflict as Ishmael is

---

[29] Sarah was actually Abraham's half sister, so his story was not entirely false. Gen. 20: 12.

generally recognized to be an ancestor of the Arab nations.[30] Isaac, according to the Bible, was the son of promise and formed the link to the impressive line of Jewish patriarchs and kings who followed. It was through this line that the *promise of the kingdom was repeatedly made.*

About 500 years later Moses was born in Egypt.[31] Fearing the large population of Jews, Pharaoh issued a decree ordering all Jewish male babies to be put to death. The baby Moses was placed in a basket sealed with pitch and bitumen and hidden in the reeds of the Nile. He was found by an Egyptian princess who raised him with the help of a Hebrew nurse who, unknown to the princess, was the child's real mother. Moses became a prominent prince of Egypt and prospered until one day he saw an Egyptian overlord abusing a Jewish worker. Moses' identity as a Jew had been revealed to him most likely by his natural mother, so he killed the Egyptian in righteous anger and hid the body. When he realized that his act had been observed, he fled in fear to Midian, where he met a daughter of the priest of Midian and married her.

Moses was living a peaceful pastoral life keeping the flock of his father-in-law, Jethro, when God spoke to him from a bush which was burning brightly but was not consumed. God's command to Moses was to go back to Egypt and free the Israelites. This was a tall order, but after resisting God for while, Moses set out for Egypt. He appeared before Pharaoh and made the request, but Pharaoh's heart was hardened. The narrative then

---

[30] God made his covenant with Isaac, but promised that Ishmael would be the father of twelve princes and make a great nation. Gen. 17:20, 21.

[31] Joseph, son of Jacob and grandson of Isaac, had been sold by his jealous brothers to Ishmaelites who carried him into Egypt. After many hardships and trials, Joseph interpreted a dream of Pharaoh and was set over all the land of Egypt second only to Pharaoh. When famine came, as the dream had predicted, Joseph sent for his brothers and his father, Jacob, thus moving the line of Jewish Patriarchs to Egypt.

recalls how God brought many plagues upon Egypt, climaxing in killing the firstborn of all the Egyptians. The angel of death passed over Jewish households, which were marked with a smear of lamb's blood. The Pharaoh, overcome with the death of his own son, then relented and let the Jews go. This great act of God in passing over the Jewish houses with the following exodus of the Jews to freedom has been celebrated ever since in a festival called the Passover.

Acting as God's agent in freeing the Israelites from slavery in Egypt was one of Moses' great accomplishments and was necessary if they were to become a nation of priests, set aside for God's purposes (including the coming of the *kingdom*).

But Moses is chiefly known as the Lawgiver. On the Jews' desert wanderings in the Sinai Peninsula, God called Moses to climb Mt. Sinai. As lightning, thunder and dark clouds swirled over the mountaintop, God gave Moses the Ten Commandments, which were written on stone tablets. He also gave Moses other laws and ordinances.[32] Moses broke the tablets asunder when he came down from the mountain and found the people reveling and worshipping a golden calf. However later, after retribution had been made, God repeated the Ten Commandments, and they were written again on stone and became the basis of a covenant between God and His people. God was clearly blessing the Israelites by giving them the Ten Commandments, God's *knowledge of good and evil* and the foundation of moral laws separating the two.

God chose the Jewish nation to proclaim His truth to the whole world. He gave them the following commission: "Now therefore, *if* you will obey my voice and keep my covenant, you shall be my own possession among all peoples; for all the earth is mine, and you shall be to me a kingdom of priests and a holy

---

[32] Ceremonial laws concerning kosher foods, cleanliness, etc.

nation."[33] And even though the rulers and nation at times failed to obey His voice, God punished them, but never disavowed them or their great purpose.

Speaking the words of the Lord as a prophet, Moses said, "I will raise up for them a prophet [Prophet] from among their brethren like you, and will put My words in his mouth; and he shall speak to them all that I command him."[34] Many interpret this prophecy as applying to the coming *Messiah (the Christ)* since, like Moses, He worked many miracles and was in such close communion with God the Father.

Moses led the people of Israel through forty years of desert wanderings but never entered the land of Canaan. God showed it to him from the top of a mountain overlooking the land. He died in Moab and was buried there. Joshua, whom Moses had laid hands on and commissioned, upon instructions from God, became the leader of Israel.[35] Following the directions of God, he led a successful invasion of the Promised Land.

After conquering the land of Canaan, Israel remained a theocracy (God, Himself, being the king) for many years before asking the Lord to give them a human king to rule over them in the manner of other nations. God gave them Saul, who reigned for many years but finally became disobedient and mentally distraught. Being displeased with Saul, God instructed Samuel, the prophet, to choose another king from among the eight sons of Jesse the Bethlehemite. After looking at the seven older sons, who were all

---

[33] Exodus 19:5, 6a RSV (my italics).

[34] Deut. 18:18 AB.

[35] Num. 27: 18-20 And the Lord said to Moses, "Take Joshua the son of Nun, a man in whom is the spirit, and lay your hand upon him; cause him to stand before Eleazar the priest and all the congregation, and you shall commission him in their sight. You shall invest him with some of your authority, that all the congregation of the people of Israel may obey."

tall and good-looking, the Lord said to Samuel, "...Man looks on the outward appearance, but the Lord looks on the heart."[36] Jesse then sent for his youngest son, David, who was tending the sheep. Like his brothers, David was also handsome. "The Lord said, 'Rise and anoint him; for this is the one.' "[37]

But David experienced many adventures and hardships before becoming king. As a lad, sent to take provisions to his brothers fighting the Philistines, he alone volunteered to fight the giant Philistine warrior Goliath, who had challenged every Israelite warrior. David, armed with only a sling, stood up to the disdainful remarks of the giant, rushed at him and with his sling sank a stone into the giant's forehead, dropping him to the ground. David then seized Goliath's sword and cut off his head. This was the first of many victories David scored over the Philistines. David became a hero to the people of Israel who came to chant, "Saul has killed his thousands, and David his ten thousands."[38] He had to flee and hide from Saul who out of jealousy was determined to kill him. David had several opportunities to kill Saul, but would not harm one who had been anointed king of Israel.

After Saul's death at the hands of the Philistines, David became king of Israel. He defeated all his enemies in battle, for God was with him. And the territory of Israel was greatly expanded.

One evening David was walking on the roof of his house when he saw a woman bathing. She was very lovely to look upon, so David, overcome with desire, inquired about her identity. He was informed that she was Bathsheba, the wife of Uriah, a faithful Israelite warrior who was fighting the Ammonites. David then sent for her and slept with her.

---

[36] 1 Samuel 16:7b AB.
[37] 1 Samuel 16:12 NRSV.
[38] 1 Samuel 18:7b NRSV.

As one unholy act leads to another, David asked his commander to put Uriah in the front ranks of the battle and then withdraw from him. Uriah was killed in the fighting. This story underscores the fact that the Bible pulls no punches, telling the whole truth about all its heroes. The prophet Nathan laid David's sin before him in a parable depicting a rich man taking the pet lamb of a poor man, slaughtering it and feeding it to his (rich man's) houseguests. David was angry with the rich man in the parable until Nathan pronounced the punch line: "You are the man."[39] David then realized he had sinned against the Lord, and he suffered much anguish.

Many Bible scholars believe that David wrote the following verses of Psalm Fifty-one as a result of this sin:

> "...For I know my transgressions,
>   and my sin is ever before me.
> Against you, you alone, have I sinned,
>   and done what is evil in your sight,
>   so that you are justified in your sentence
>   and blameless when you pass judgment..."[40]

Part of the retribution for David's sin was the death of his first son by Bathsheba. Other family problems persisted in the revolt of his son, Absalom, who was killed by one of David's men in the struggle that followed.

Even though David committed this serious sin, his life consisted of carrying out God's purposes for Israel, and his memory is cherished by the Israelites, who idealize his victories and his reign over Israel. David was such an ideal king that the prophet, Nathan, spoke the words of the Lord to him, "Your house and your *kingdom* shall be made sure forever before me; *your*

---

[39] 2 Samuel 12:7 NRSV.
[40] Psalm 51:3,4 NRSV

throne shall be established forever."[41] (Joseph, the husband of Mary, mother of Jesus, was descended from David through twenty-eight generations. Mary's linage also went back to David.)   This prophecy foreshadowed the coming of the *kingdom* of God, with David, an ideal king, foreshadowing the great *Messiah* to come.

David's faith in the Lord is what sustained his whole life. His words before the assembly of Israel clearly reveal that faith. "Therefore David blessed the Lord in the presence of all the assembly; and David said: 'Blessed art thou, O Lord, the God of Israel our father, for ever and ever. Thine, O Lord, is the greatness, and the power, and the glory, and the victory, and the majesty; for all that is in the heavens and in the earth is thine; thine is the *kingdom*, O Lord, and thou art exalted as head above all.' "[42]

----

1. Who is considered to be the founding father of Israel?
2. What great quality did God see in this man?
3. What promise did God make to this founding father?
4. Why did Moses leave Egypt? And why did he return?
5. What commission did God give to the Jewish nation?
6. What sin did David commit?   What were the consequences?

Recommended reading: Genesis 11:26-32,12:1-9
Genesis 15:1-6
Genesis 17:1-8, 15, 16
Exodus 2:11-15
Exodus 3:1-14

---

[41] 2 Samuel 7:16 NRSV (my italics).
[42] 1 Chr. 29:10,11 RSV (my italics).

Exodus 12:1-14
Exodus 19:2-8a
Exodus 20:1-17
2 Samuel 7:16,17

Three

Israel, Unique Among Nations

The development of the ancient nation of Israel provided the only culture and religion out of which the concepts of *Messiah* and the *kingdom* of God could come. Theologically speaking, God elected this people to make Himself and His purpose known both to Israel and eventually to the rest of the world. This point is made perfectly clear in the book of Genesis when the patriarch Abraham was directed by God to leave the pagan land of his fathers and travel to an unknown land which God would give to him and his offspring. As previously stated, the promise to Abraham was not only that he would become the father of many nations, but that the nations of the earth would be *blessed* by him and his seed.

Outside of Israel, mankind struggled literally in the dark, inventing a multiplicity of "gods" to explain and make sense of life. Many were nationalistic "gods" with strange names. Statues were erected and temples built to enshrine them, but always their characters were simply super egos of the people who invented them. Although pictured larger than life, they exhibited bad tempers, struggles for power, and lust— just like their human counterparts.

By the faith of Abraham and his descendants, a new nation unencumbered by pagan gods and practices was developed. Right at the start an agreement called a covenant, more binding than a legal contract, was established between Abraham (and his descendants) and God. Unlike a legal contract, this covenant was to last forever and it set forth the conditions under which the community of Israel as well as the individual would thrive: recognizing and obeying the one and only God and having faith in His promises of blessings. Other covenants would follow between Israel and God, emphasizing and spelling out their special relationship.

Much of the Old Testament is the story of how this relationship played out in what is called "salvation history." The covenant would be renewed by Israel after great deliverances such as the exodus from Egypt and the return from exile in Babylon. Finally, Jeremiah prophesied that God would make a *new covenant* with the house of Israel and the house of Judah. This *new covenant* would not be like the old ones, which the people broke. "...I will put my law within them, and I will write it upon their hearts; and I will be their God and they will be my people...I will forgive their iniquity, and I will remember their sin no more."[43] The coming *Messiah* would be God's Instrument in establishing this *new covenant*.

The nation was founded by a holy, righteous and mighty God, who created the heavens and the earth and who alone is immortal. It was rescued and sustained by this God and also punished when it strayed from the covenant and the Law. The relationship between God and every Israelite was paramount and (in addition to the covenant) was best described by the Shema: "Hear, O Israel: the Lord our God is one Lord, and you shall love the Lord your God with all your heart, and with all your soul, and

---

[43] Jeremiah 31:33b, 34b RSV.

with all your might. And these words which I command you this day shall be upon your heart; and you shall teach them diligently to your children, and shall talk of them when you sit in your house, and when you walk by the way, and when you lie down and when you rise."[44]

The Ten Commandants formed the heart of the moral Law,[45] and the importance of this basic subject was addressed as follows, "And now, Israel, what does the Lord your God require of you, but to fear the Lord your God, to walk in all his ways, to love him, to serve the Lord your God with all your heart and with all your soul, and to *keep the commandments and statutes of the Lord...*"[46]

Since God played such a paramount part in the history and culture of Israel, and since the principles of right and wrong were embedded in God's commandments, disobedience had to be dealt with. The tabernacle had been built during the desert wanderings after the exodus from Egypt. It was designed according to God's specifications, and in the book of Leviticus instructions were given concerning animal sacrifices to atone for sin.

To the nation God was altogether "holy", and the covenant demanded that his people be holy. In addition to moral purity, holiness carried the meaning of being set aside for God's use. Any one or any thing set aside for God's use had to be "clean." Offenses committed against a member of the community were also offenses against a holy God and reparations had to be made to those offended. Furthermore, the offender had to "cleanse himself" and set himself right with God, which required an animal sacrifice. The basic concept was that sin was transferred to the animal, which then died in place of the sinner who deserved to die for breaking the covenant. It was specified that the animal be without blemish and that the shedding of the animal's blood

---

[44] Deut. 6:4-7 RSV.

[45] There were also ceremonial laws, which addressed sacrifices, tithes, offerings, cleanliness, etc.

[46] Deut. 10:12,13a RSV (my italics).

would "cover" the sin and cleanse the sinner. The sinner's guilt would also be assuaged and the community made whole or holy again.

Several types of sacrifice are described in Leviticus. Many, however, deal with some particular type of sin or misdeed which had to be recognized and addressed. Once a year on the Day of Atonement, two goats were brought to the tabernacle, one of which was slaughtered. The High Priest would take some of its blood into the most holy place inside the curtain and sprinkle some of it on the mercy seat.[47] He would then lay both his hands upon the head of the other goat and confess all the iniquities, transgressions and sins of the people. This goat would be led off into the wilderness and set free. The goat would bear all the iniquities of the people and go away into a barren place. The "scapegoat" would thereby atone for the sins of the whole nation and would put the people back into a right relationship with God and the covenant until the following year on the next Day of Atonement.

Much has been written about whether animal sacrifices could cover anything but unintentional sin. The Hebrew word translated *unintentional* could have other meanings.[48] For the most serious, deliberate, and unrepentant sins a person would be "cut off" from the community or considered outside the commonwealth of Israel. Animal sacrifice alone could not atone for such sins. The Psalms speak of a deep repentance directed to God.[49] This concept is developed further in the prophets and in the coming of the *Messiah*.

---

[47] By this he would make atonement for the sanctuary for all the sins of the people. The mercy seat was the golden covering on the Ark of the Covenant. It was regarded as the resting place of God and was kept in the most holy place in the Tabernacle.

[48] Hebrew word *saga* could mean to wander or go astray (with knowledge of the Law) like simply lapsing occasionally rather than sinning unintentionally.

[49] See Psalm 51.

1. What is a covenant? What part did it play in the establishment of Israel?
2. Explain the covenant prophesied by Jeremiah. How would this covenant be established?
3. How was lapsing or unintentional sin dealt with in ancient Israel? Explain the meaning of the word, *holy*, to the nation of Israel.
4. What is the Shema? Describe how it summarized the relationship of the Israelite to God.
5. Describe the Day of Atonement. How did this sacrifice relate to the Christ?
6. Discuss how the uniqueness of Israel throughout history has an impact on us today.

Recommended reading: Genesis Chapter 15
                     Jeremiah 31:31-36
                     Leviticus Chapter 4
                     Leviticus 6:1-7
                     Deuteronomy 6:1-15
                     Leviticus 16:1-22
                     Hebrews 9:1-15

Four

The Prophets of Israel

After the deaths of David and his successor son, Solomon, the Kingdom of Israel began a steady decline and bickering led to a division of the country with Israel in the north and Judah in the south. Some of their kings followed the ways of the Lord, but many did evil in His sight. Both small nations were thereafter constantly threatened by the powers of Assyria, Babylon, Greece and Rome. In 722 BC Israel was conquered by Assyria. In 587 BC Babylon conquered Judah with many of its leading citizens taken into exile. The *kingdom* of God seemed to be a remote and nebulous concept, the return to the Garden a far away and lost ideal.

The only bright spot during this time were the words of the prophets of Israel and Judah. Prophets were special people chosen by God to speak His words. Quite often the words applied to the contemporary period and also to the future.[50] The prophets spoke the truth to kings and common people and raised hopes by promising the coming of the *Messiah* and the *kingdom* of God. They also warned the people to return to the Lord and practice justice and mercy. Most spoke of the last days of earth, when natural disturbances and disasters would strike the earth and the judgment of God would come swiftly.

Daniel, Zechariah, and Isaiah are three of the prophets whose words speak clearly about the coming of the *Messiah* and the *kingdom* of God.

Daniel was one of the young Jews taken into captivity to Babylon. His writings cover much of the seventy years of the Babylonian exile. He came to the attention of King Nebuchadnezzar by his interpretation of the King's dream. This occurred when none of the magicians, sorcerers or diviners of the King could either tell the King his dream or interpret it. God revealed the dream and its interpretation to Daniel, who gave the answer to the king, thus saving the lives of all the wise men of Nebuchadnezzar's court.

The dream had consisted of a giant statue, with different metals, gold, silver, bronze and iron comprising parts of its body. Its feet were made of iron and potter's clay. The different metals represented various kingdoms which would dominate their times. Significantly, at the end of the dream, a Stone was cut out "without human hands." The Stone smashed the feet of the image and then the rest until the bits and pieces were carried away by the wind. Daniel revealed that the Stone was the *kingdom* of God, which in the final days would smash all earthly kingdoms and would *stand forever*.

---

[50] Just as bifocal lenses allow the reader to see near when reading and far off, prophesy is bifocal, allowing the interpretation to be contemporary as well as applying to the future.

The King, greatly impressed with this revelation, rewarded Daniel with gifts and made him ruler over the province of Babylon and head over all the wise men. In addition, the King was in great awe over the power of Daniel's God, admitting that He was God of gods and Lord of kings. Daniel continued to serve the King and the Babylonian government, but he never let any matter come ahead of his worship and obedience to God. He is considered one of the greatest moral and spiritual figures of the Old Testament and is called a man greatly esteemed by God. Daniel showed his first loyalty to God in many ways even when he became entangled with other Babylonian functionaries who were jealous of the great rank bestowed upon him. In each of these trials he was vindicated because God was with him.

In one of Daniel's night visions, "on the clouds of the heavens came One like a Son of man, and He came to the Ancient of Days and was presented before him. And there was given Him [the Messiah] dominion and glory and kingdom, that all peoples, nations, and languages should serve Him. His dominion is an everlasting dominion which shall not pass away, and His kingdom is one which shall not be destroyed."[51]

Another intriguing prophecy in Daniel is the seventy weeks of years. According to the New American Standard Bible, the passage reads as follows:

> "Seventy weeks have been decreed for your people (the Jews) and your holy city (Jerusalem), to finish the transgression, to make an end of sin, to make atonement for iniquity, to bring in everlasting righteousness, to seal up vision and prophecy and to anoint the most holy *place.*
>
> "So you are to know and discern *that* from the issuing of a decree to restore and rebuild Jerusalem until Messiah the Prince *there will be* seven weeks

---

[51] Daniel 7:13,14 AB.

and sixty-two weeks; it will be built again with plaza and moat, even in times of distress.

"Then after the sixty-two weeks the Messiah will be cut off and have nothing, and the people of the prince who is to come will destroy the city and the sanctuary."[52]

This passage could be one of the most astounding in Scripture. Interpreting each week to mean 7 years as we find expressed in another place in the Old Testament,[53] we can follow the prophecy's fulfillment. Artaxerxes, king of Persia, issued the decree in the twentieth year of his reign in the month of Nissan (April).[54] The year would have been about 445 BC according to history. Adding seven weeks of years and sixty-two weeks of years gives us 483 years. That date would coincide with the year of Christ's crucifixion and even the month, April.[55] In 70 AD, a number of years after the crucifixion, the Romans (people of the prince to come) under the general, Titus, destroyed Jerusalem.

It is no wonder that the church fathers placed the Book of Daniel with the other prophets of Israel. They believed that God spoke to the prophets and for that reason future events could be

---

[52] Daniel 9:24,25,26a NASB (my parenthesis).

[53] Genesis 29:27 NASB Also the word for weeks, *shabua*, in Hebrew can mean simply "seven."

[54] Nehemiah 2:1-8 RSV.

[55] Sir Robert Anderson, celebrated Chief of Criminal Investigation, Scotland Yard, made this determination using a 360 day- year in his book, *The Coming Prince*. In ancient Mediterranean times a solar year was considered to be 360 days or 12 months of 30 days. By the most meticulous scholarship, using the best accepted authorities of his day, Anderson showed 32 A.D. as the year of the crucifixion of Jesus. He then wrote: "What then was the length of the period intervening between the issuing of the decree to rebuild Jerusalem and the public advent of '*Messiah* the Prince'—between the 14th of March, B.C. 445, and the 6th April. A.D. 32? The interval contained exactly to the very day 173,880 days, or seven times sixty-nine prophetic years of 360 days, the first sixty-nine weeks of Gabriel's prophecy."

predicted. This prophecy predicts with remarkable accuracy the *coming of the Christ* and the events following. After the crucifixion, God began to deal primarily with the church of Jesus Christ in order to spread the good news of the Gospel. Thus the seventieth week of the prophecy *about the Jewish people* was interrupted and will commence with the coming of the Antichrist and the tribulation.[56] These "last days" events according to the Book of Revelation will take seven years.

Zechariah prophesied at the end of the Babylonian exile as the Jews were returning to Jerusalem, which in the book is the City of God, the center of God's manifestations. The book is difficult to understand because it is a series of visions and oracles, which include some repetition. Zechariah encourages the builders of the temple, but warns the people to listen to the Lord and practice honesty, justice, mercy and compassion. The first real glimpse into the future comes as the prophet speaks of the Branch, who will build the true temple of the Lord. "...It is He Who shall build the [true] temple of the Lord, and He shall bear the honor *and* glory [as of the only begotten of the Father] and shall sit and rule upon His throne. And He shall be a Priest upon His throne, and the counsel of peace shall be between the two [offices—Priest and King]."[57]

However, one very important condition had to be met before the *Messiah* could bring in the *kingdom*. Sin had to be dealt with, a function of the Priest-King. Mankind had not been able to accomplish this, so it was up to God to do that which was beyond man's capacity. Zechariah tells us that God "will remove the iniquity and guilt of this land in a single day."[58]

---

[56] The period of time spoken of by all the prophets when God's wrath will be poured out upon the earth, making life almost insufferable.
[57] Zech. 6:13 AB.
[58] Zech. 3:9b AB.

All the prophets agree that no impure person will enter the *kingdom* of God, and Isaiah sets the record straight when he says, "All we like sheep have gone astray, we have turned each one to his own way;..."[59] Or as the Psalmist says, "They have all gone astray, they are all alike perverse; there is no one who does good, no, not one."[60] If this is true, the *kingdom* will have no meaning for sinful mankind. The first objective of the *Messiah* must be to lift the fog bank of sin, which had blinded mankind since the expulsion from the perfect Garden. God sent Jesus to do just this—to take away our sin. Consequently, He did not enter Jerusalem as a conqueror on a white horse, but in the same way that Zechariah had prophesied four hundred years earlier:

> "Rejoice greatly, O Daughter of Zion! Shout aloud, O Daughter of Jerusalem!   Behold, your King comes to you; He is [uncompromisingly] just and having salvation [triumphant and victorious], patient, meek, lowly, and riding on a donkey, upon a colt, the foal of a donkey." [61]

Jesus knew that rejection, torture, and a most agonizing death were ahead. This was the cup that Jesus hated to swallow, but He did it for it was the perfect will of His Father. It was the only path to fulfilling His work on earth. He sweated real drops of blood in contemplating it. His apostles tried to talk Him out of it. When the moment of crisis drew closer, He resolutely chose to carry it out.

Jesus, the *Messiah*, was indeed rejected by his own people, who in so doing, acted for *all* people (who had gone astray each one to his own way—the way of the world). He took upon himself the sin of his people *and* the sin of the world even though he had led a perfect life. He was whipped until he no longer resembled a man

---

[59] Isa. 53:6a AB.
[60] Psalm 14:3 NRSV.
[61] Zech. 9:9 AB.

and then nailed to the cross. During a brief moment, He was forsaken by God, the Father, until He had poured his life out as a sacrifice for sin.

Zechariah states it this way, "Awake, O sword, against My shepherd and against the man who is My associate, says the Lord of hosts; smite the shepherd and the sheep [of the flock] shall be scattered..."[62]

The essential task of taking away the sin of the world was indeed accomplished by Jesus Christ in one day, making it possible for all who received Him to be reconciled with God, to repent and be forgiven and to earnestly expect to enter the *kingdom* of God. We can now pray with joy, "Thy *kingdom* come, Thy will be done in earth as it is in heaven." [63] For those saved by Christ's mighty act, the *coming of the kingdom* is an event to look forward to—to be energized in God's service—not an event to hide from and fear.

The *Second Coming* will be to complete the establishment of the *kingdom*, to judge all souls and to usher back in the wonders of the Garden, paradise regained. According to Zechariah, the armies of many nations will come and surround Jerusalem. The Lord will descend from Heaven to fight against His foes, and the great victory of the Lord will usher in the *kingdom*. When the Israelites recognize the Lord, (Whom they had rejected), there will be a great wailing:

> "And it shall be in that day that I will make it my aim to destroy all the nations that come against Jerusalem. And I will pour out upon the house of David and upon the inhabitants of Jerusalem the Spirit of grace *or* unmerited favor and supplication. And they shall look [earnestly] upon Me Whom

---

[62] Zech. 13:7a AB.
[63] Matt. 6:9 KJV (my italics).

they have pierced, and they shall mourn for Him as one mourns for his only son and shall be in bitterness for Him as one who is in bitterness for his firstborn."[64]

Zechariah also makes it plain that the *kingdom* is not just for the people of Jerusalem and Israel but for all who acknowledge Christ and receive Him. "And everyone who is left of all the nations which came against Jerusalem shall even go up from year to year to worship the King, the Lord of hosts..."[65]

Paschal Lamb, by God appointed,
All our sins on thee were laid;
By almighty love appointed,
Thou hast full atonement made.
Every sin may be forgiven,
Through the virtue of Thy blood;
Opened is the gate of heaven;
Peace is made twixt man and God.[66]

----

1. What happened to Israel after the reigns of David and Solomon?
2. Describe the main themes proclaimed by the prophets of Israel.
3. What was the dream which Daniel told and interpreted for the King of Babylon? How did the dream end?
4. What outstanding problem had to be dealt with before the *Messiah* could bring in the kingdom of God?

---

[64] Zech. 9:9 AB.
[65] Zech. 14:16a AB.
[66] Second verse of a hymn most likely by John Bakewell (1721-1819)

5. Who is the *Branch* Zechariah speaks about? What two functions will this figure have?
6. How is it that Jesus atoned for the sins of the whole world?
7. Is there evidence of His redemption in our broken world? Is his forgiveness inherent in your everyday life?

Recommended reading: 1 Kings 11:1-11
          1 Kings 11:26-40
          Daniel 2:31-45
          Daniel 7:9-14
          Zechariah 3:8,9
          Zechariah 7:8-14
          Zechariah 9:9,10
          Zechariah 13:7
          Zechariah 12:7-10
          Matthew 26:30,31

Five

The Prophet Isaiah, Herald of the Christ

Many people have called the Book of Isaiah the Gospel of the Old Testament. This is because Isaiah prophetically describes the role of the *Messiah, the coming Christ,* in such vivid and graphic terms. The description is not only of a wonderfully wise counselor and majestic king, but also of one who bears the sins and iniquity of the people, making atonement for their sins, and reconciling them to God.

Can you imagine living in the time of Isaiah or in one of the dozens of generations between Isaiah and the coming of the Christ? The writings of the prophets would be all that could sustain you. Chapter nine begins with a momentous announcement of greatest importance:

> "In the former time he brought into contempt
> the land of Zebulun and the land of Naphtali, but
> in the latter time he will make glorious the way of
> the sea, the land beyond the Jordan, Galilee of the
> nations. *The people who walked in darkness have seen a*

great light, those who lived in a land of deep darkness—on them the light has shined...For a child has been born for us, a son given to us; authority rests upon his shoulders, and he is named Wonderful Counselor, Mighty God, Everlasting Father, Prince of Peace. His authority shall grow continually and there shall be *endless peace* for the throne of David and his *kingdom.* He will establish and uphold it with justice and with righteousness *from this time onward and forevermore.* The zeal of the Lord of hosts will do this."[67]

The messianic figure is from Galilee. He is larger than life, more than a mere human being. What He does (bringing the people out of darkness) will be *endless* and *forevermore* and the zeal of the Lord of Hosts will accomplish it. What a wondrous event to look forward to! A further reading of the prophet reveals a more detailed description of this messianic figure:

"A shoot shall come out from the stump of Jesse (the father of David), and a branch shall grow out of his roots. The spirit of the Lord shall rest on him, the spirit of wisdom and understanding, the spirit of counsel and might, the spirit of knowledge and the fear of the Lord. His delight shall be in the fear of the Lord. He shall not judge by what his eyes see, or decide by what his ears hear; but with righteousness he shall judge the poor and decide with equity for the meek of the earth; he shall strike the earth with the rod of his mouth, and with the breath of his lips he shall kill the wicked. Righteousness shall be the belt around his waist, and faithfulness the belt around his loins."[68]

---

[67] Isa. 9:1b,2,6,7 NRSV (my italics).
[68] Isa. 11:1-5 NRSV (my parenthesis).

The next few chapters relate the history of the times including the miraculous saving of Jerusalem from a huge Assyrian army. Assyria was the principal world power of the Mediterranean area at that time. Their army had been marauding the countryside of Judah and was now surrounding Jerusalem, poised for the attack. Isaiah had warned the king of Judah against relying on foreign alliances for protection. He continued to advise the king to trust in the Lord for the protection of Jerusalem, but the king was not that trusting. In spite of the king's lack of faith, Isaiah prophesied that the Lord would strike the large Assyrian army with such force that they would have to return home. In the course of one day a plague struck the Assyrian force, killing 185,000 warriors. Such was the fulfillment of Isaiah's prophecy, with the Assyrian army withdrawing.

A new section starts with Chapter 42 where again a larger than life figure is introduced. He is God's Servant. "Behold My Servant, Whom I uphold, My elect in Whom My soul delights! I have put My Spirit upon Him; He will bring forth justice *and* right *and* reveal truth to the nations…"[69] The Lord further declares that He has called His Servant for a righteous purpose and that He will be a *covenant to the people of Israel* and a light to the Gentile nations. "It is too light a thing that you should be my servant to raise up the tribes of Jacob and to restore the survivors [of the judgments] of Israel; I will also give you for a light to the nations, that My salvation may extend to the end of the earth."[70] The Servant will be called to open the eyes of the blind and to bring out prisoners from the dungeons. The Lord announces that He is now declaring *new things* before they come to pass.

Isaiah (and his disciples), prophesying from the eighth into the seventh century BC, had earlier predicted the Babylonian exile and captivity. Now he predicts that a Persian king named Cyrus will rise up, conquer Babylon and free the Jews to return to their

---

[69] Isa. 42:1 AB.
[70] Isaiah 49:6 AB.

homeland. This event took place in 539 BC when Cyrus, conqueror of Babylon, issued his decree freeing the Jews from captivity.

In Chapter 50 we hear directly from the figure called the Servant, Who indicates for the first time in Isaiah that He must suffer. "[The Servant of the Lord says] The Lord God has given me the tongue of a disciple and of one who is taught, that I should know how to speak a word in season to him who is weary...The Lord has opened My ear, and I have not been rebellious or turned backward. I gave my back to the smiters and My cheeks to those who plucked off the hair; I hid not My face from shame and spitting. For the Lord God helps Me; therefore have I not been ashamed or confounded. Therefore have I set My face like a flint, and I know that I shall not be put to shame."[71]

This same theme is picked up again in the last verses of Chapter 52 when the prophet states that the Servant's face and whole appearance will be marred more than any man's. However, He will startle many nations, and rulers will shut their mouths because of Him. Kings will see and hear that which they have not known and they shall understand.

Then comes the heart of the prophecy, Chapter 53, which most closely predicts in remarkable detail the coming of the Christ, Who is one and the same with the Servant:

> For [the Servant of God] grew up before Him like a tender plant...
> He was despised and rejected and forsaken by men, we did not appreciate His worth or have any esteem for Him.
> Surely He has borne our griefs (sicknesses, weaknesses, and distresses) and carried our

---

[71] Isa. 50:4a,5,6,7 AB.

sorrows and pains [of punishment], yet we [ignorantly] considered Him stricken, smitten and afflicted by God....

But He was wounded for our transgressions; He was bruised for our iniquities; the chastisement [needful to obtain] peace and well being for us was upon Him and with the stripes [that wounded] Him we are healed and made whole.

All we like sheep have gone astray, we have turned every one to his own way; and the Lord has made to light upon Him the guilt and iniquity of us all.

He was oppressed [yet when] He was afflicted, He was submissive and opened not His mouth; like a lamb that is led to the slaughter, and as a sheep before his shearers is dumb, so He opened not His mouth. By oppression and judgment He was taken away; He was cut off out of the land of the living [stricken to His death] for the transgression of my [Israel's] people, to whom the stroke was due?

And they assigned Him a grave with the wicked, and with a rich man in His death, although He had done no violence, neither was any deceit in his mouth. Yet it was the will of the Lord to bruise Him;...When You and He make His life an offering for sin [and He has risen from the dead, in time to come]

He shall see his [spiritual] offspring. He shall prolong His days, and the will *and* pleasure of the Lord will prosper in His hand. He shall see [the fruit] of the travail of his soul and be satisfied; by His knowledge of Himself [which he possesses and imparts to others] shall My [uncompromisingly] righteous One, My Servant, justify many and make many righteous (upright and in right standing with God) for He shall bear their iniquities and their guilt [with the consequences, says the Lord].[72]

This passage was written approximately 700 years before the coming of Jesus. I remember obtaining the translation of Isaiah found in the Dead Sea Scrolls. The language has changed very little as compared with today's KJV or the RSV of the Bible. If I ever had any doubts about the ability of the prophets to hear God and predict the future, they were erased. That the passage applies to Jesus the Christ cannot be doubted either. The prophet Isaiah goes to great length describing time after time the sins of the people of Israel, also spoken of as a servant (little "s") of God. *The Servant* on the other hand is always described as My righteous One in whom God delights. He is also described as One Who was wounded specifically for the transgression of Israel's people, as well as for the transgression of all people.

Chapter 61 opens with the words Jesus read at the synagogue in Nazareth:

"The Spirit of the Lord God is upon me, because the Lord has anointed *and* qualified me to preach the Gospel *of* good tidings to the meek, the poor, *and* afflicted; He has sent me to bind up *and* heal the broken hearted, to proclaim liberty to the [physical and spiritual] captives and the opening of the prison *and* of the eyes to those who are bound. To proclaim the acceptable year of the Lord [the year of his favor] and the day of vengeance of our God, to comfort all who mourn."[73]

---

[72] Isa. 53:2a,3,4,5,6,7,8,9,10,11 AB.

[73] Isa. 61:1,2 AB.

After the reading, Jesus then made a startling announcement, "Today this scripture has been fulfilled while you are present *and* hearing."[74] *The Christ was coming into a world of people who did* not *recognize Him or know Him,* but Isaiah proclaims that "the Lord God will cause rightness *and* justice and praise to spring forth before all the nations [through the self-filling power of His word]."[75]

Isaiah closes this spectacular book of prophecy with the pronouncement of the coming of the *kingdom* of God. "For behold, I create new heavens and a new earth."[76]   This is a statement John echoed hundreds of years later in the book of Revelation. Isaiah's description of the new creation follows and although it is not as sweeping and complete as John's, there is no doubt about what is being described. Even though the center of this new creation is in Jerusalem, the City of God, it is plain that it is for all who will come, see, and accept God's glory. The following evangelistic passage makes that clear: "And the time is coming when I will gather all nations and tongues, and they will come and see my glory. And I will set up a [miraculous] sign among them, and from them I will send survivors to the nations…to the isles *and* coastlands afar off that have not heard of my fame nor seen My glory. And they will declare *and* proclaim My glory among the nations."[77]

God, however, is no universalist. All people will not be saved and there will be a day of vengeance for both Jews and Gentiles who have rejected His justice, righteousness and sovereignty. According to Isaiah, God describes the man who pleases Him: "But this is the man to whom I will look and have regard: he who is humble and of a broken or wounded spirit, and who trembles at My word and reveres My commands."

---

[74] Luke 4:18,19 AB.

[75] Isa. 61:11b AB.

[76] Isa. 65: 17a AB.

[77] Isa. 66: 18b,19 AB.

My soul chases after many things in this life,
My soul seeks its real home in this life.
My soul longs for, is desperate for the real, the satisfying experience of life.
My soul seeks, chases, pursues many avenues of pleasure, self-fulfillment, gratification, excitement.
All these fall short—even though they might provide momentary satisfaction: a happy and fulfilling marriage, children and grandchildren,
Wonderful expressions of love and projection of personality.
Travel to new and far away, even exotic places, hobbies pursued to endless perfection,
Looking for the perfect home, dwelling where my soul can feel contentment,
Legitimate pursuit of wealth, even pursuit of ways to help others.
All of these might provide some degree of fulfillment and yet all fall a little short,
Until we finally discover that the One God sent, in whose person He, Himself, came to us, alone can satisfy.
For it is in Christ that we find our perfect fulfillment, our perfect home, our greatest sense of righteousness. He alone satisfies all our human desires and goals. And each experience of his sublime presence and reality brings us closer to the heart of God,
Moves us closer to our real home. [78]

----

1. Early in Isaiah, the prophet announces the coming of the *Messiah*. From what region will He come? From what family (by human perception) will he be descended?
2. For what purpose will the Servant come? Quote the passage which describes the inclusive scope of the Servant's role.
3. Find the passage in which Isaiah first indicates that the Servant must suffer.

---

[78] Author's reflections.

4. What are the specific prophecies in Chapter 53 that apply to the Christ?

5. In Chapter 61 we find the scripture that Jesus read aloud to a congregation. Name the congregation. What results followed?

6. Reflect upon how the Suffering Servant, the *Messiah*, brings about our redemption.

Recommended reading: Isaiah 9:1-7
                      Isaiah 11:1-10
                      Isaiah 50:4-9
                      Isaiah 52:13 through Chapter 53
                      Isaiah 61:1-3
                      Luke 4:14-30
                      Isaiah 65:17 through Chapter 66:2
                      Luke 24: 44-47

Six

Christ in the Book of Psalms

We don't usually think of the *Messiah* being mentioned in the Psalms. But like the prophets of Israel who spoke both to the present and the future in almost the same breath, the Psalms speak of David, an anointed of the Lord, and in more sublime language shift immediately to the *Anointed* of the Lord, the *Messiah*. For example, in Psalm 16:

> "For You will not abandon me to Sheol (the place of the dead), neither will You suffer Your holy one [Holy One] to see corruption."[79]

On the other hand, Psalm 2 speaks exclusively of the *Messiah*. It speaks of the nations banding together against God:

> "Why do the nations assemble with commotion [uproar and confusion of voices], and why do the people imagine (meditate upon and devise) an empty scheme?

---

[79] Psalm 16:10 AB.

The kings of the earth take their places;
the rulers take counsel together against the
Lord and His Anointed One (the Messiah, the
Christ). *They say,*

Let us break Their bands [of restraint]
and cast Their cords [of control] from us.

He Who sits in the heavens laughs; the
Lord has them in derision [and in supreme
contempt He mocks them].

He speaks to them in His deep anger and
troubles (terrifies and confounds) them in His
displeasure and fury, *saying,*

Yet have I anointed (installed and placed)
My King [firmly] on My holy hill of Zion.

I will declare the decree of the Lord: He
said to Me, You are My Son; this day [I declare]
I have begotten You.

Ask of Me, and I will give You the
nations as Your inheritance, and the uttermost
parts of the earth as Your possession..."[80]

The language calling the anointed *my Son,* together with the
expression, *I have begotten You,* makes it clear Who is spoken of.
Also the extreme statement that the Lord will give his Son the
uttermost parts of the earth indicates a reference to the *kingdom* which
Christ will rule.

Remembering the expression in Daniel concerning a *stone cut
without human hands,* we find in Psalm 118 another reference to the
stone:

"The stone which the builders rejected has
become the chief cornerstone. This is from the
Lord and is His doing; it is marvelous in our eyes.
This is the day that the Lord has brought about;
we will rejoice and be glad in it....Blessed is he
who comes in the name of the Lord."[81]

---

[80] Psalm 2:2-8 AB.
[81] Psalm 118:22-24,26a AB.

In another one of David's psalms, 110, he speaks about the
Messiah—about a priest-king:

> "The Lord (God) says to my Lord (the
> Messiah) Sit at My right hand, until I make Your
> adversaries Your footstool. The Lord will send
> forth from Zion the scepter of Your strength;
> rule, then, in the midst of Your foes....The Lord
> has sworn and will not revoke *or* change it; You are
> a priest forever, after the manner *and* order of
> Melchizedek."[82]

Finally, we see in Psalm 22 a prophetic portrait of the
crucifixion of Christ in realistic detail. Although it is probably
David who is speaking, the graphically related experience is not
one of David's. And though David was hounded by Saul and
went through some harrowing experiences, he was never put
through the horror described here:

> "But I am a worm and not a man,
> A reproach of men and despised by the people.
> All who see me sneer at me;
> They separate with the lip, they wag the head, *saying,*
> 'Commit *yourself* to the Lord; let Him deliver him;
> Let Him rescue him, because He delights in him.'..."
> They open wide their mouth at me,
> As a ravening and a roaring lion.
> I am poured out like water.
> And all my bones are out of joint;
> My heart is like wax;
> It is melted within me.
> My strength is dried up like a potsherd,
> And my tongue cleaves to my jaws;

---

[82] Psalm 110:1,2,4 AB. After defeating several kings to save his nephew,
Lot, Abraham was blessed by Melchizedek, King of Salem (later Jerusalem).
Abraham gave him a tithe of all he had taken in the battle. Gen. 14:14-24.

And You lay me in the dust of death.
For dogs have surrounded me;
A band of evildoers have encompassed me;
They pierced my hands and my feet.
I can count all my bones;
They look and stare at me;
They divide my garments among them,
And for my clothing they cast lots."[83]

This same psalm opens with the words of Jesus on the cross, "My God, my God, why have You forsaken me?" And it closes with the last words of Jesus before He died, "It is finished." The closing passage is a rousing and ringing exclamation of vindication and victory:

> "All the ends of the earth shall remember and turn to the Lord, and all the families of the nations shall bow down *and* worship before You...
> Posterity shall serve Him; they shall tell of the Lord to the next generation.
> They shall come and shall declare His righteousness to a people yet to be born—that He has done it [that it is finished]!"[84]

This Psalm clearly prophesies the crucifixion of *Christ* in very graphic detail as well as telling of His ultimate reign throughout the world. As far as the *kingdom* is concerned, it should be understood by now that the *final coming of Christ and the establishment of the kingdom* are really one and the same.

Other short portions of the psalms are quoted in the Gospels, but those discussed in this chapter are quoted again and again, signifying their true prophetic and messianic content.

---

[83] Psalm 22:6-8, 13-18 NASB (my italics).
[84] Psalm 22:27,30,31 AB.

You alone, O Christ, can gladden our hearts.   You alone can satisfy our deepest yearnings.   It is not enough to work hard and be successful.   Our souls find satisfaction in the spiritual, in the divine, in an eternity we can believe in and eventually enter.[85]

----

1. David was an anointed of God—just as Jesus is *the* anointed of God.   In Psalm 2, what phrases lead one to conclude the psalm is really about the Christ?
2. Compare the stone in Daniel 2:34 with the stone in Psalm 118. Then look up Matthew 21:42, Acts 4:11, and 1 Peter 2:7.
3. In what Psalms does David speak about the *Messiah?*
4. In what specific ways does Psalm 22 speak of Jesus?

Recommended reading: Psalm 2
                     Acts 4:23-31
                     Psalm 16
                     Acts 2:22-30
                     Psalm 110
                     Acts 2:29-36
                     Psalm 22
                     Matthew 22:41-45
                     Luke 23:32-37

---

[85] Author's reflections.

Part Two

New Covenant and Fulfillment

Seven

The Kingdom Collides with Earth

There are very few really earth shaking events in the history of this planet. I might suggest some—such as Creation, bringing forth the human race, or expulsion from the Garden of Eden. Others might select discovery of the "new world," cracking of the atom or the flight of the spacecraft, Discovery. But all these would pale in light of the *really big one.*

After the last half of the fifth century BC, the voice of prophets was heard no more in the land. During the next four hundred years the nation of Israel was reduced to a small province subject to each advancing empire. Huge armies marched across the face of the Mediterranean world. The era was one of military might making right, as first the Persian Empire prevailed, followed by the Greeks led by Alexander the Great. Finally the greatest of them all, the Roman Empire stretched from North Africa to England.

It was Roman policy to allow a reasonable amount of local autonomy, so even though the Roman governor had the last word,

Israel retained a figure-head king and a tolerated religious establishment. A political-religious council called the Sanhedrin possessed very limited powers. Jews were divided into two main parties: the Pharisees, who saw themselves as strict practitioners of the Law and traditions of Judaism, and the Sadducees, who were more worldly and friendly with the Romans. On the periphery were the Essenes, who led a strict, monastic type life and worshipped apart in their own separate communities. The temple in Jerusalem, however, was the recognized center of Jewish worship and teaching.

Spiritually, the world was dark. Only a small flickering light in Judah could be seen and even it appeared to go out from time to time. But at such times the faint breath of the prophets seemed to blow across the embers igniting a small flame. That small flame was the hope of Israel and (unknown to others) the hope of the world— and that hope was the coming *Messiah*, the *Christ* of God. It was not uncommon for an Israelite with a small band of followers to make the claim of *Messiah*, the anointed one. But just as hopes arose, they were quickly dashed; the pretender was exposed as he failed to fulfill prophetic expectations.

It was in the nation of Israel that mankind had begun to come in out of the dark. But the Law was not enough. It was difficult to follow, and when violated, animal sacrifices were made day after day, year after year, to take away the sins of the people.[86] Something *greater* was needed, and the answer was to be found in the message of the prophets. Some in Israel still believed in this coming move of God and were awaiting it. According to the prophets this event would challenge Creation and all other events in importance and value to the human race. It would remove the blight of sin and open the gates of the Garden once again to mankind.

---

[86] See Hebrews 10:1-4.

For many Jews, the chosen people of God, four hundred years of subjugation was just too much and some began to cry, "How long, O God, must we wait?" But just when the interminable night appeared darkest, God acted. It was not the awesome explosion of a huge meteor crashing to earth. It did not come in the form of fire and smoke swirling around a mountain top. It was not a charismatic military leader rising to crush Rome. A child was born...not in a palace or a dwelling or even an inn...but in a stable.

There were, however, some fireworks after all. The Scripture tells us that angels appeared in the sky singing, "Glory to God in the highest..." And a little later a procession of wise men from the East came to worship the child and bring Him gifts. Even so, for the vast majority of Israelites, nothing had really happened; nothing had changed. Who would prepare the way for the coming *Messiah?*

There was a man named John living in the wilderness. He wore a rough garment of camel's hair with a leather girdle. His food was what he could extract from the desert, mainly consisting of locusts and wild honey. In no way would he have been considered attractive to Jews who were living the easy life, yet there was a compelling quality to his speech. He spoke with a divine conviction and poured out his wrath especially upon leaders of the Pharisees and Sadducees and called all his listeners to repentance. Some compared him to the prophet Elijah while others recalled the words of Isaiah, "The voice of one crying in the wilderness: Prepare the way of the Lord, make his paths straight."[87]

All who were truly moved to confession and repentance, he baptized in the Jordan River. Some were even asking if he could be the *Messiah* to which he quickly replied, "I baptize with water to

---

[87] Isaiah 40:3.

wash away your sins, but a mightier one is coming after me who will baptize you with fire and the Holy Spirit."

John's reputation grew and soon people from Jerusalem and all over Judea were coming to be baptized. Jesus, the child born in the stable, had grown to full manhood, working with his earthly (foster) father, Joseph, in a carpenter's shop. One day he came from his home in Galilee to be baptized by John. To the few who knew him, he was simply a carpenter, the son of Mary and Joseph of Nazareth. So he waited his time in line and his appearance before John caused no special stir or interest among the people.

But John's piercing glare saw something more and so as he baptized him, he shouted, "Look! There is the Lamb of God, Who takes away the sin of the world![88] For John had seen the Spirit of God descend like a dove and remain upon Jesus. And a voice from heaven was heard saying, "This is my beloved Son, with whom I am well pleased."[89] This sign had been revealed to John earlier by God.

There had been previous signs concerning Jesus. According to Holy Scripture, when his mother, Mary, was still a virgin engaged to Joseph, the angel Gabriel appeared to her saying, "Hail, O favored one, the Lord is with you!... you will conceive in your womb and bear a son and you shall call his name Jesus. He will be great, and will be called the Son of the Most High; and the Lord God will give to him the throne of his father David, and he will reign over the house of Jacob forever; and of his kingdom there will be no end."[90]

But Mary stammered, "How can this be? I have as yet no husband."

---

[88] John 1:29b AB.
[89] Matt.5:17 RSV.
[90] Luke 1:28b, 31b, 32, 33 RSV.

The angel replied, "The Holy Spirit will come upon you, and the power of the Most High will overshadow you; therefore the child to be born will be called holy, the Son of God."[91]

There was a man in Jerusalem named Simeon. He was righteous and devout and looking for the deliverance of Israel. The Holy Spirit came upon him and revealed that he would not die before he had seen the Lord's Christ, the Messiah. Simeon came into the temple when Joseph and Mary brought Jesus to be presented to the Lord,[92] *He took the baby into his arms and said, "Lord, now lettest thou thy servant depart in peace, according to thy word; for mine eyes have seen thy salvation which thou hast prepared in the presence of all peoples, a light for revelation to the Gentiles, and for glory to thy people Israel."* [93]

And so with the baptism by John and the anointing of the Holy Spirit, Jesus began His[94] public ministry. The Scripture records His first public words, "Repent, for the *kingdom of heaven* is at hand!"[95]

The promise made to Abraham that his seed would bless all nations was being fulfilled. As Paul later wrote, "…that in Christ Jesus the blessing of Abraham might come upon the Gentiles, that we might receive the promise of the Spirit through faith…And if you are Christ's, then you are Abraham's offspring, heirs according to promise."[96]

----

[91] Luke 1:35b RSV.

[92] Luke 8:22,23. Every firstborn Jewish male was presented to the Lord one month after birth.

[93] Luke 2:29-32 RSV.

[94] I have capitalized the pronouns referring to Jesus after the Holy Spirit descended upon Him and John recognized the Son of God. The RSV and NRSV quotations never capitalize the pronouns.

[95] Matt. 4:17b RSV (my italics).

[96] Gal. 3: 14, 29 RSV.

1. Describe the situation around the Mediterranean after the last half of the 5th century BC. What was missing in Israel during the next 400 years?
2. What was the baptism of John? How did it differ from that baptism Jesus would bring?
3. Name three signs of the coming *Messiah*.
4. Explain how the promise of God to Abraham was fulfilled.
5. Discuss the divinity and humanity of Jesus.

Recommended reading: John, 1:1-34
                      Luke 1: 26-35
                      Matthew 1:17-25
                      Luke 2:22-35
                      Matthew Chapter 3

Eight

The Revolutionary Ministry of Christ

Jesus began His public ministry as an itinerant teacher or rabbi. But it soon became evident that He was much more than a teacher. The Scripture tells us that, "...He went about all Galilee teaching in their synagogues and preaching the gospel of the *kingdom* and healing every disease and every infirmity among the people. So his fame spread throughout all Syria, and they brought him all the sick, those afflicted with various diseases and pains, demoniacs, epileptics, and paralytics, and he healed them. And great crowds followed him from Galilee and the Decapolis and Jerusalem and Judea and from beyond the Jordan."[97] The world had never witnessed anything like the ministry of Jesus.

There was much more. When He read from the prophet Isaiah in the synagogue in Nazareth, He took upon himself a profound destiny—one that would change the world or in the words of His enemies concerning his disciples: one that would turn the world upside down.[98] In the words of Paul, "He (God)

---

[97] Matt.4:23-25 RSV (my italics).
[98] See Acts 17:6b

has delivered us from the dominion of darkness and transferred us to the *kingdom* of his beloved Son, in whom we have redemption, the forgiveness of sins."[99] Jesus' message could not be taken casually. Neither could it be ignored. The choices He presented were matters of life and death—not just life in this world but life in eternity.

As His ministry moved forward, His role became clearer. I have always loved the directness and sincerity of the expression of Andrew, "We have found the Messiah."[100] Or that of Philip, "We have found him of whom Moses in the law and also the prophets wrote…"[101] And that of Nathanael, "Rabbi, you are the Son of God! You are the King of Israel!"[102] And Peter in answer to a question posed by Jesus concerning his identity, "You are the Christ, the Son of the living God."[103] Peter again, after the teaching of Jesus about the Bread of Life, "And we have learned to believe and trust and [more] we have come to know [surely] that You are *the Holy One of God*, the Christ (the Anointed One), the Son of the living God."[104]

Almost from the start as it remains today, His message and ministry stirred up either intense love and devotion or jealousy and hatred. Just as the prophets had done before Him, He attacked sham, pretense, and hypocrisy particularly on the part of religious leaders. And He spent time with sinners, which in the eyes of the Pharisees, was dealing with those who had put themselves outside the Commonwealth of Israel. He healed on the Sabbath, which to the legalistic Pharisees was a fracture of the Law.

---

[99] Col. 1: 13, 14 RSV (my italics and parenthesis).
[100] John 1:41 RSV.
[101] John 1:45 RSV.
[102] John 1:49 RSV.
[103] Matt. 16:16 RSV.
[104] John 6:69 AB.

When His hand was called on some questions of the Law, He showed an intellectual prowess that repudiated and baffled the lawyers, Scribes, and Pharisees. His extraordinary insight caused them to ask such questions as: where did this man who has no education get all this knowledge? "And they were amazed at His teaching, for His word was with authority *and* ability *and* weight *and* power."[105]

The main reason Jesus came was to save sinners, to take away the sin of the world so that we could be reconciled to God, receive forgiveness and salvation and be admitted to His *kingdom.* Jesus once said, "And I, when I am lifted up from the earth, will draw all men to myself."[106] He said this, knowing by what kind of death He was going to die. After living the perfect life and teaching the perfect word of God, He offered up his own body as the perfect sacrifice and substitute for our sins—for all sins of mankind from the beginning to the end of the age. He thereby fulfilled the prophecy of Isaiah and Zechariah, paid the price a holy God requires for *our* sins, and opened the way to eternal life in the *kingdom* of God for all repentant believers. The Baptist's appellation, "the Lamb of God who takes away the sin of the world" proved to be quite accurate.

Just as the Jewish system of sacrifices eventually became as much a ritual as an expiation of sin, the Christian church today in the technically advanced nations has made compromises with the more radical teachings of Christ. Many of these compromises began as an effort to adjust to the morality and standards of society (society's concept of good and evil). When that happens the church always loses its appeal and spiritual authority until its influence grows very weak or even ceases to exist. On the other hand, the goals and worldly rewards of a technologically advanced

---

[105] Luke 4:32 AB.
[106] John 12:32 RSV.

society begin to take precedence, and the voice of the true Gospel grows fainter and fainter.

In the next two chapters, I would like to stress some of the fundamental teachings of Christ. As always, they will be controversial, but Jesus warned us openly that this would happen. And as He said, "Not everyone who says to me, 'Lord, Lord,' shall enter the *kingdom* of heaven, but he who does the will of my Father who is in heaven."[107]

Jesus! The name that charms our fears, that bids our sorrows cease,
'Tis music in the sinner's ears; 'tis life, and health, and peace.
He speaks, and listening to His voice, new life the dead receive;
The mournful broken hearts rejoice; the humble poor believe.
Hear Him, ye deaf; His praise, ye dumb, your loosened tongues employ;
Ye blind, behold your Savior come; and leap ye lame, for joy.[108]

----

1. What distinguished the ministry of Jesus from others who claimed to be the *Messiah*?
2. How was the message of Jesus comparable to that of the prophets of Israel?
3. What did Jesus offer to those who genuinely accepted Him and received the Holy Spirit?
4. Explain how Jesus took away the sin of the world.
5. Why do you think that the message of Jesus is growing weaker in the technically advanced Western countries and making great advances in some third world countries?

Recommended reading: Matthew Chapter 4

---

[107] Matt. 7:21 RSV (my italics).
[108] The 3rd, 5th, and 6th verses of a hymn written by Charles Wesley in 1749 entitled, "O for a Thousand Tongues to Sing."

Luke 5:1-26
John 3:1-21
Matthew 26:17-29
Galatians 3:23-Chapter 4:7

Nine

Christ and the Law of Moses

Some in our society have called the Beatitudes "the impossible ethic." Yet these simple but very direct statements form a perfect prologue to Christ's discussion of the Law. Blessed will be those who are poor in spirit, who mourn, the meek and those who hunger after righteousness. Also blessed will be the merciful and the pure in heart, the peacemakers and those who are persecuted for righteousness' sake.[109]

The Law given to Moses and later clarified by the prophets was one of God's greatest gifts to his chosen people. Although it was difficult to keep, it set a standard of behavior for the nation of Israel to strive for. It also set the nation apart from other nations to become "holy", for God's use. In the Gospel of Matthew, Jesus, who was reared with a wholesome Jewish heritage, elevates and fulfills the Law of Moses, completing God's gift of defining good and evil and revealing it for all mankind.

---

[109] Based on Matt. Chapter 5.

Jesus said, "Think not that I have come to abolish the law and the prophets; I have come not to abolish them but to fulfill them. For truly I say to you, till heaven and earth pass away, not an iota, not a dot will pass from the law until all is accomplished....he who does them and teaches them shall be called great in the *kingdom* of heaven."[110] After making His attitude toward the Law clear, Jesus then begins to clarify what He means by fulfilling it.

You shall not kill. Whoever kills shall be liable to judgment. *But I say whoever is angry with his brother shall be liable to judgment. Also whoever insults his brother or calls him a fool shall be liable to judgment or hell.*

You shall not commit adultery. *But I say everyone who looks at a woman lustfully has already committed adultery in his heart.*

Whoever divorces his wife shall give her a certificate of divorce. *But I say to you that whoever divorces his wife except for unfaithfulness makes her an adulteress and he who marries a divorced woman commits adultery.*

You shall not swear falsely. *But I say to you, do not swear at all. Give a simple yes or no.*

You have been taught, an eye for an eye and a tooth for a tooth. *But I say to you, do not resist one who is evil. If he should strike you on the right cheek, turn the left to him also. Give to one who begs and lend to one who would borrow.*

You shall love your neighbor and hate your enemy. *But I say to you love your enemies and pray for those who persecute you.*

Rounding out the discussion of the Law are several commandments pointing the way to salvation:

---

[110] Matt. 5:17,18,19b RSV (my italics). RSV does not capitalize law and prophets.

*Do not store up for yourselves treasure on earth, but lay
up for yourselves treasure in heaven where it will be safe in
your heavenly account. For where your treasure is, there
also will be your heart.*

*Do not be anxious about tomorrow. Let the day's own
problems be sufficient for the day.*

*Do not judge and condemn others so that you might not
be treated likewise.*

*Enter by the narrow gate for the gate is wide and the
way easy that leads to destruction.*

*The gate is narrow and the way hard that leads to life.
Few will find it.* [111]

Later in His ministry Jesus speaks of the last judgment. When
the nations are brought before the Son of Man's throne to be
judged, He separates the sheep from the goats. He tells the sheep
to *inherit the kingdom* prepared for them. He says that when He was
hungry, they gave Him food. When He was thirsty, they gave
Him drink and when He was a stranger, they welcomed Him.
When He was naked, they clothed Him and when He was sick,
they visited Him. When He was in prison, they came to Him.
Surprised, they asked Him, "When did we do these things for
You?" And He answered, "When you did it unto the least of
these, you did it unto Me."[112] This passage illustrates in a positive
way the standard of compassion and mercy which will be required
of any who seek to enter the *kingdom* of God.

---

[111] This whole passage is based upon Matt. Chapters 5, 6, 7.

[112] Based on Matt. Chapter 25. Some interpret this passage as applying to the
nations that come to the aid of Israel as the actual translation reads, "…unto
the least of these, *My brethren*…"

The Law of Moses has become the basis of law for many civilized nations, and yet the world is experiencing arguably more lawlessness than ever before. *Why?* First, the fulfilling of the Law set forth by Jesus has never been fully adopted. But more importantly, even though the Law was a necessary taskmaster to prepare the nation of Israel and other nations for God's use, *it could not change the heart.* That could only be done by God's direct intervention as foretold by the prophets. Jesus spoke of fulfilling the Law *and the Prophets.* Or as Paul put it, "...God has done what the law, weakened by the flesh, could not do."[113] That action of God consisted of giving his only begotten Son to take away the sin of the world. As John wrote in the opening to his Gospel, "For the law was given through Moses; grace and truth came through Jesus Christ."[114] To the extent that Christ has been received, God's commandments have been written on the heart.

Again and again, you called us to return. Through prophets and sages you revealed your righteous Law. And in the fullness of time you sent your only Son, born of a woman, to fulfill your Law, to open for us the way of freedom and peace.

By his blood, he reconciled us,
By his wounds, we are healed.[115]

----

1. Describe Jesus' basic attitude toward the Law.
2. In what way did Jesus "change" the Law? Be specific in regard to one's enemies and in regard to "an eye for an eye and a tooth for a tooth."

---

[113] Rom. 8:3a RSV.
[114] John 1:17 RSV.
[115] *The Book of Common Prayer, 1979* p. 370.

3. Point out the ways Jesus also elevated the qualities of mercy and compassion.
4. The Law was God's instrument for training Israel and other nations. What more did God have to do to change the heart?
5. Is the Sermon on the Mount an impossible ethic? Why or why not?

Recommended reading: Matthew Chapter 5
                      Matthew Chapter 6
                      Matthew Chapter 7
                      Matthew 25:14-46
                      Romans 7:14 through 8:11
                      Romans 12:9-21
                      Hebrews 10:1-25
                      Acts 13:38-41

Ten

He Turned the World Upside Down

There is no question that the teachings of Jesus upset some long held practices and traditions of mankind. Many people were dismayed. One of the paramount teachings of Jesus is about the danger of striving for riches and material goods. Since the attainment of riches has always been one of the top goals of mankind, the following teaching is important to remember.

One day a rich young man came up to Jesus and asked what he must do to inherit eternal life. After rehearsing the commandments with him, the young man said, "I have always observed these, what do I still lack?" Jesus answered, "Go, sell all that you possess. Give it to the poor so your treasure will be in heaven and come and follow me." Upon hearing this, the young man turned away very sorrowfully for he had great possessions.

Jesus then addressed his disciples, "It will be hard for a rich man to enter the *kingdom* of heaven.[116] In fact it is easier for a camel to go through the eye of a needle than for a rich man to enter the *kingdom* of God."[117] After warning about paying too much attention to material possessions, Jesus told a parable about a farmer. The farmer's crops yielded so plenteously that he had no place to store the surplus. So he decided to tear down his barns and build bigger ones to hold all his grain and goods. After doing this, he said to himself, "Soul, you have ample goods for years to come. Take it easy—eat, drink, and be merry." But that night God said to him, "Fool! This night your soul is required of you. What now will become of your goods? Whose will they be?" So it will be for one who lays up for himself treasures and is not rich toward God.[118]

The problem Jesus addresses is not aimed at prosperity so much as at the covetousness of those persons who place the

---

[116] After writing this chapter, my thoughts turned inward for several days. I actually began to wonder just how well I had followed the requirements of the Lord. I would certainly not classify myself as being *rich*, but I have never really wanted for anything from a material standpoint. Most of my life I have tithed my income to the church and other Christian endeavors. I have also supported numerous worthwhile causes and charities. But what about the needs of people close around me, in my church family and in my circle of friends and acquaintances?

Then I began to see needs that should be met. Perhaps that's a lesson the Lord has allowed me to learn from my own writing. I remembered how my father met the needs in his community. He hired handicapped workers and if they couldn't make the grade, he gave them a job which fit their ability— however limited. He put several businessmen back on their feet when they faced impossible problems. He worked one half of every day for months at our area's medical center when it was without a director. He supported relatives in need, and I never once heard him take any credit for these deeds. Maybe some people think that kind of giving is old-fashioned. Maybe I did at one time, but I don't now.

[117] This and the preceding paragraph are based on Matt.19:16-24.
[118] Based on Luke 12:18-21.

greatest importance upon worldly riches and whose time, energy, and effort is directed primarily toward attaining wealth and keeping it. Wordsworth said it in one of his poems: "The world is too much with us; late and soon, getting and spending, we lay waste our powers...." [119] Jesus puts it bluntly, "No man can serve two masters; for either he will hate the one, and love the other; or else he will hold to the one, and despise the other. Ye cannot serve God and mammon."[120]

And Jesus continued, "Therefore I tell you, stop being perpetually uneasy (anxious and worried) about your life, what you shall eat *or what you shall drink*; or about your body, what you shall put on. Is not life greater [in quality] than food, and the body [far above and more excellent] than clothing?"[121]

Jesus said, "Give to him who begs from you, and do not refuse him who would borrow from you....Beware of practicing your piety before men in order to be seen by them, for then you will have no reward from your Father who is in heaven."[122]

In the parable of the sower, the seed that fell among thorns is like "others who hear the Word; Then the cares and anxieties of the world and distractions of the age, and the pleasure and delight and false glamour and deceitfulness of riches, and the craving and passionate desire for other things creep in and choke and suffocate the Word and it becomes fruitless."[123]

The positive side of this question is given by Jesus in the Gospel of Matthew, "...do not be anxious...For the Gentiles seek all these things; and your Heavenly Father knows that you need them all. But seek first his *kingdom*, and his righteousness, and all

---

[119] "The World Is Too Much With Us; Late And Soon" by William Wordsworth (1770-1850).
[120] Matt. 6:24 KJV.
[121] Matt. 6:25 AB.
[122] Matt. 5:42; 6: 1 RSV.
[123] Mark 4:19 AB.

these things shall be yours as well."[124] Wasn't that turning the culture around a bit?

The world has always been a competitive place. Struggling to get to the top has been a principle pursuit of mankind.

The wife of Zebedee, mother of two of Jesus' disciples, John and James, approached Jesus one day. Like most mothers she was anxious to see her sons get ahead. The request she made of Jesus was, "Give instructions that my two sons will sit, one on your right hand and one on the left when You come into your *kingdom*." Jesus quickly replied that it was not for Him to decide but for his Father. And then He called all his disciples to Him and said, "You know that the leaders of the Gentiles hold sway over their people and keep them in subjection. It will not be so with you for whoever wishes to be great among you must be your servant, and whoever desires to be first among you must be your slave. Just as the Son of Man came not to be served but to serve and even give His life as a ransom for many.[125]

On another occasion a rigorous discussion took place about what it means to be a disciple. Jesus explained that whoever gives up his life in this world for the sake of the Gospel will save it in the *kingdom* of God. He then said, "For what does it profit a man to gain the whole world, and forfeit his soul or his life in the eternal *kingdom* of God?"[126]

Once again the disciples asked Jesus who is the greatest in the *kingdom* of heaven. Jesus called a little child to Himself and said, "Whoever will humble himself therefore and become like this little

---

[124] Matt. 6:31, 32 RSV (my italics).
[125] Based on Matt.20:25-28.
[126] Based on Mark 8:36.

child [trusting, lowly, loving, forgiving] is greatest in the kingdom of heaven."[127]

One day when Jesus was teaching, probably in Peter's house, His mother and brothers came and standing outside, called for Him. When He was given this message, He looked around the room and said, "See! Here are My mother and My brothers; For whoever does the things God wills is My brother and sister and mother!"[128]

Many of these teachings are *fulfillments* of the Jewish Shema which instructs the Jews to love the Lord, their God, with all their heart, with all their soul, and with all their might. Jesus' summary of the Law coupled the Shema with the directive to love your neighbor as yourself and carried the authoritative statement that all the Law and the Prophets hang on these two commandments.[129]   His fulfillment of the law carried the commandments to a much higher level, but also carried mercy to that level as well. We remember that He said, "So be merciful (sympathetic, tender, responsive and compassionate) even as your Father is [all these]."[130] The culture of every age seems to lag sadly in the qualities of love (agape), mercy, and humility.

Jesus said, "I thank you, Father, Lord of heaven and earth, that You have concealed these things [related to salvation] from the wise and understanding and learned, and revealed them to babes (the childlike, unskilled, and untaught). Yes, Father, for such was Your gracious will *and* choice *and* good pleasure."[131]

---

[127] Matt. 18:4 AB.
[128] Mark 3: 34b. 35 AB.
[129] Matt. 22:36-40.
[130] Luke 6: 36 AB.
[131] Luke 10:21b AB.

"Woe to you, (Jesus said) when all men speak well of you, for so their fathers did to the false prophets."[132]

The Pharisees were highly respected and looked up to. When they heard Jesus talking about the pitfalls of wealth, they began to scoff and laugh, but Jesus who knew how much they loved money and how covetous they were, said to them, "You are the ones who declare yourselves just and upright before men, but God knows your hearts. For what is exalted and highly thought of among men is detestable and abhorrent (an abomination in the sight of God.)"[133]

One day Jesus sat in the Temple watching people cast money into the treasury. The rich were putting in large sums. When a poverty stricken widow came and put in two copper mites, He said: "This widow has put in more than all the rest, for they gave out of their abundance, while she, in her poverty, has put in everything that she had—even all that she had to live on."[134]

But perhaps the greatest gulf between worldly culture and what Jesus taught is in the realm of repentance, forgiveness, and the attitude toward one's enemies. The Pharisees could not understand the association of Jesus with sinners. This led Jesus to say, "...there will be more joy in heaven over one [especially] wicked person who repents (changes his mind, abhorring his errors and misdeeds, and determines to enter upon a better course of life) than over ninety-nine persons who have no need of repentance."[135]

---

[132] Luke 6:26 RSV (my parenthesis).
[133] Luke 16:15 AB.
[134] Based on Mark 12:41-44.
[135] Luke 15:7 AB.

Jesus ate with sinners because He said that He came to save and heal them—that those who are well have no need of a physician. He saved the woman accused of adultery by telling her accusers, "Let him who is without sin, cast the first stone."[136] He then told her to go and sin no more. He commended the tax collector who was contrite and confessed his sins over the Pharisee who thanked God he was not like other men.

Concerning one's enemies, Jesus said, "Invoke blessings upon and pray for the happiness of those who curse you, implore God's blessing (favor) upon those who abuse you [who revile, reproach, disparage, and highhandedly misuse you.]"[137] This was a major culture turn around.

Continuing on this theme, Jesus said, "...If anyone wants to sue you and take your undershirt (tunic), let him have your coat also. And if anyone forces you to go one mile, go with him two [miles]."[138]

Jesus took the doctrine of forgiveness to a much higher plane than Judaism. He said, "And whenever you stand praying, if you have anything against anyone, forgive him *and* let it drop (leave it, let it go) in order that your Father Who is in heaven may also forgive you your (own) failings and shortcomings *and* let them drop. *But if you do not forgive, neither will your Father in heaven forgive your failings and shortcomings.*[139]

---

[136] Based on John 8:7
[137] Luke 6:28 AB.
[138] Matt. 5:40, 41 AB. Roman soldiers could force people of subjugated nations to walk a long distance assisting with each soldier's load or baggage. Therefore the saying was difficult for the Jews.
[139] Mark 11:25, 26 AB.

When Peter asked Jesus how many times he should forgive a brother, Jesus replied seventy times seven (or an infinite number of times).

The parable of the prodigal son illustrates how much God loves his creatures and how fervently He wants to forgive and receive them back. After the prodigal son had received his portion of money, he went to a foreign country squandering his property in loose living. When he had spent it all, he got a job feeding swine, and his hunger almost drove him to eat the pods the swine ate. So he said, "I will arise and go to my father, and I will say to him, 'Father, I have sinned against heaven and before you, I am no longer worthy to be called your son; treat me as one of your hired servants.' " His father saw him coming a long way off. He rejoiced and ordered a feast to be held for his wayward son.

Later when the other brother (who had always been obedient and trustworthy) asked about the appropriateness of this response, the father said, "It was fitting to make merry and be glad, for this your brother was dead, and is alive, he was lost, and is found." The father greatly loved his sons just as the heavenly Father loves all his children and receives the repentant back with great joy.[140]

We remember that as He was being nailed to the cross, Jesus said, "Father, *forgive* them; for they know not what they do."[141] Later in His instructions to the disciples, Jesus said that repentance and forgiveness of sins should be preached in His name to all nations, beginning from Jerusalem.[142]

It is important also to recognize that the sacrifice of Jesus followed the Jewish sacrificial rite of imposing the sins of the person(s) upon a perfect animal and slaying the animal in place of

---

[140] Based on Luke 15.
[141] Luke 23:34 RSV (my italics).
[142] Luke 24:47 RSV(my cap. on *His*)

the sinner, thereby expiating the sin (the sin being forgiven by God). The perfect sacrifice by Jesus ended the necessity for animal sacrifices as the sacrificial victim was the Son of God, Himself, and that expiation is sufficient for all people for all times to come[143] (a definite cultural change).

Even after all the healings and miracles, the God-given teachings and the perfect life of Jesus, the scribes and Pharisees' biggest complaint was His *forgiving* sins, His claim to be God's Son.[144] This complaint constituted the major charge brought against Jesus by the leaders of the Jews, who testified to the Romans that He was guilty of setting Himself against Caesar and stirring up the people. Pilate, the Roman governor, was not persuaded, but reluctantly gave the order for Jesus' crucifixion. He did this primarily to please the Jewish leaders and the crowd which they had assembled.

He died that we might be forgiv'n
He died to make us good,
That we might go at last to heav'n
Saved by His precious blood.

There was no other good enough
To pay the price of sin;
He only could unlock the gate
Of heav'n and let us in.[145]

---

[143] Hebrews 9:12; 10:10.
[144] Mark 2: 5-7 RSV. "And when Jesus saw their faith, he said to the paralytic, 'My son, your sins are forgiven.' Now some of the scribes were sitting there, questioning in their hearts, 'Why does this man speak thus? It is blasphemy! Who can forgive sins but God alone?'"
[145] Third and fourth verses of a hymn by Cecil Frances Alexander (1818-1895).

1. Why, according to Jesus, will it be difficult for a rich man to enter the kingdom of God?
2. How do you interpret the words of Jesus when he said to give to one who begs and lend to one who desires to borrow?
3. How do we seek first the kingdom of God? Do we really believe that when we follow this principle that "these other things will be added to us?"
4. Jesus said that the greatest among us will be the servant or slave of all. How does this saying fit into our competitive society?
5. It is sometimes difficult to remember to pray for our friends. Can we really pray sincerely for our enemies?
6. What will happen to us if we cannot forgive those who persecute us and treat us wrongfully?
7. Is the culture we live in truly a Christian culture?

Recommended reading: Luke Chapter 6
                      Mark Chapter 10
                      Matthew 20:1-28
                      Luke 23:1-25
                      Acts 17:1-9
                      1 Corinthians 1:26-31

Eleven

The End of the Beginning

It was the day after the crucifixion of Jesus, ordered by Roman authorities and carried out by Roman soldiers, who had pierced His hands and His feet and cast lots for His clothing. The Jewish religious leaders had put away the Teacher's threat to their authority and position. The scattered band of Jesus' disciples was in hiding and Mary, His mother, and the other women were in deep mourning. Night came and seemed to last forever. But God was not nearly through.

At daybreak the next morning the muffled sound of women's voices could be heard as Mary Magdalene and another woman approached the sepulcher where Jesus had been laid. The soldiers guarding the tomb seemed to be asleep on their feet. Strangely, the large stone which sealed the entrance had been rolled aside, and when the women looked in, the body of Jesus was not there. Neatly folded in a pile, the grave clothes lay on the stone shelf. The head covering was also neatly rolled up at the other end.

While they stood perplexed, two men in dazzling raiment appeared to them and said, "Why do you seek the living among the dead? He is risen from the dead just as He said."

After this, events flowed swiftly. The chief priests were seized with fear and anxiety. The apostles were astonished and even a little skeptical. This feeling dissipated rapidly when Jesus began appearing to them even when they were behind closed doors. His instructions to the disciples were clear, "All authority in heaven and on earth has been given to me. Go and make disciples of all nations, baptizing them in the name of the Father, and of the Son, and of the Holy Spirit, teaching them all I have commanded you, and lo, I am with you always, to the close of the age."[146]

Before He departed, Jesus told them that before many days they would be baptized with the Holy Spirit, Who would give them *power* from on high. All this happened just as He said it would. The one-day Jewish festival of Pentecost was celebrated fifty days after the major feast of Passover. The time was also approximately fifty days after the resurrection of Jesus. Many Jews from the eastern end of the Mediterranean were in Jerusalem for the festival. The Apostles were sitting together in the upper room. Some were praying and others were contemplating the instructions of Jesus when suddenly a violent rushing wind swept through the house. Immediately tongues of flame appeared in their midst, separated and settled on each one of them. And they were filled to overflowing with the Holy Spirit of God.

They left the house and entered the street speaking in foreign languages. A crowd, hearing the tornado-like noise, had also gathered in the street. There were Jews from many different countries, but each one heard the Apostles, enabled by the Spirit, speaking in his own native language. Recognizing the Apostles as Galileans, the crowd was amazed and bewildered. Peter, with the eleven standing beside him, addressed the people with a stirring speech about the crucifixion, death, and resurrection of Jesus

---

[146] Matt. 28:18,19 RSV.

Christ. When he stated that God had made Jesus, whom they had crucified, Lord and Christ, many in the crowd were stung to the heart and asked what they must do to be saved. Peter replied, "Repent, and be baptized every one of you in the name of Jesus Christ for the forgiveness of your sins; and you shall receive the gift of the Holy Spirit. For the promise is to you and to your children and to all that are far off, every one whom the Lord our God calls to him."[147] The Scripture tells us that about three thousand souls were baptized and added to the Way that day.

And so as these miraculous events unfolded, instead of being the disastrous end of Jesus' ministry, it became the glorious end of the beginning of God's move to offer salvation to all mankind.

After the Holy Spirit had come upon the disciples, Peter and John were entering the temple one day. They came upon a man crippled since birth. When the lame man asked alms of them, Peter replied that they had no gold or silver, but they would give him what they had. Peter then said to the man, "In the name of Jesus Christ of Nazareth, walk."[148] And he took him by the hand and raised him up, and immediately his feet and ankles grew strong. The former lame man then entered the temple, walking and leaping and praising God. This was the first of all the healings brought about by the disciples and many others in the ages that followed, all done in the name of Jesus.

This amazing miracle attracted much attention and the people flocked to Peter, who made the following speech: "Men of Israel, why do you wonder at this, or why do you stare at us, as though by our own power or piety we had made him walk. The God of Abraham, and of Isaac and of Jacob, the God of our fathers, glorified his servant Jesus, whom you delivered up and denied in

---

[147] Acts 2:38, 39 RSV.
[148] Act 3: 6b RSV.

the presence of Pilate, when he had decided to release him. But
you denied the Holy and Righteous One, and asked for a
murderer to be granted to you, and killed the Author of life,
whom God raised from the dead. To this we are witnesses. And
his name, by faith in his name, has made this man strong whom
you see and know; and the faith which is through Jesus has given
the man this perfect health in the presence of you all.

"And now, brethren, I know that you acted in ignorance, as did
also your rulers. But what God foretold by the mouth of all the
prophets that his Christ should suffer, he thus fulfilled. Repent
now, and turn again, that your sins may be blotted out, that times
of refreshing may come from the presence of the Lord..."[149]

It is well to recall this speech, which is just as true and fresh
today as it was in the time of Peter. It marked the continued
ministry of Christ on earth, manifesting itself in healings,
deliverances, and conversions, effected through the power of the
Holy Spirit in the name of Jesus the Christ.

I know that my Redeemer lives:
What joy the blest assurance gives!
He lives, He lives, who once was dead;
He lives, my everlasting Head!

He lives to bless me with His Love;
He lives to plead for me above;
He lives my hungry soul to feed;
He lives to help in time of need.

He lives and grants me daily breath;
He lives and I shall conquer death;
He lives my mansion to prepare;

---

[149] Acts 3: 12b-19 RSV.

He lives to bring me safely there.[150]

----

1. On the third day, who came first to the tomb where Jesus had been laid? Describe the inside of the tomb.
2. Upon hearing that the tomb was empty, describe the feeling of the Apostles. Describe the feeling of the Chief Priests. What would have been your feeling?
3. After the coming of the Holy Spirit, what miracle occurred as Peter and John were entering the temple? Do these types of miracles still occur in the name of Jesus?
4. Do you believe that Jesus Christ is the same, yesterday, today, and forever? Comment upon.
5. Can you think of any incidents in your life which you could describe as miraculous? Explain.

Recommended reading: Mark 15:1-Chapter 16
　　　　　　　　　　　Luke Chapter 24
　　　　　　　　　　　Acts Chapter 2, Chapter 3
　　　　　　　　　　　Acts 4:29-31
　　　　　　　　　　　Revelation 1:4-18

---

[150] First, second and third verses of a hymn by Samuel Medley (1738-1799).

Twelve

The Full Meaning of the First Coming

We must always remember that on earth Jesus was an ardent Jew. All of His disciples were also Jews. Even Paul, whom many believe was educated in a Gentile university,[151] was the most fervent Pharisee of his day. We can not fully understand why almost all of the Jewish religious and political leaders rejected Jesus. The primary traditional reason is that the Jews expected the *Messiah* to be a larger than life king who would overthrow the Romans and rule on the throne of David forever. There is ample reason for this point of view. The prophets other than Isaiah and Zechariah primarily pictured the kingship and ruling aspect of the Christ. Even the first portion of Isaiah emphasizes this thought. This aspect of the *Messiah* will definitely appear with the *Second Coming.*[152]

---

[151] University at Tarsus. Later it is believed that he attended the rabbinical school of Gamaliel.

[152] Jesus, himself, said, "For like the lightning, that flashes and lights up the sky from one end to the other, so will the Son of Man be in His (own) day. But He must suffer many things and be disapproved and repudiated and rejected by this age and generation." Luke 17: 24, 25 AB.

Another reason for the attitude of prominent Jews would lie in the threat Jesus posed to their position. They knew the authenticity of His healings; they respected His inspired teachings. They felt threatened by His following among the people. Some of them felt the Romans would crack down hard if the people tried to make Him king. And there was the fact that Jesus many times had exposed their failings and even their hypocrisy. What place would they have if Jesus became king?

This fear of Jesus had existed since His birth when Herod had ordered all the male children in Bethlehem up to two years old to be killed.[153] I believe most of the feeling generated against Jesus originated from this fear. That includes the many efforts to ask Him trick questions in the presence of His followers, a tactic used to undermine His authoritative teachings. So the chief priests and the Pharisees convinced the Roman governor, on trumped up charges, to crucify Him. The rulers of the Jews thereby rejected His role as God's *Messiah*.

But the record of history belies such a point of view. Jerusalem fell to the Roman armies just as Jesus had predicted.[154] This took place in 70 AD not very long after His crucifixion. The power of the Holy Spirit[155] took over His followers, who came to

---

[153] See Matt. 2:16.

[154] See Matt. 24:2.

[155] Author's note: In this book I have chosen to emphasize two themes: the *Messiah* and the *kingdom* of God. The great importance of the role of the Holy Spirit must always be understood. Jesus began His ministry after the Spirit descended upon Him at His baptism. The coming of the Holy Spirit upon the disciples at Pentecost was the beginning of the fearless evangelistic fervor of the Christian Church. People are saved after receiving the Lord, Jesus Christ, when the power of the Spirit comes upon them. The Scriptures makes it abundantly clear that we must be born of the Spirit and not just of the flesh in order to be saved. St. Paul perhaps puts it best, "If the Spirit of him who raised Jesus from the dead dwells in you, he who raised Christ from the dead will give life to your mortal bodies also through his spirit that dwells in you." Romans 8:11 NRSV.

have no fear either of the Romans or the prominent Jews. The most powerful, intellectual Jew of his day, Paul, was converted from the harshest enemy of Christ to the greatest evangelist and theologian of his age.   Under the influence of the Spirit, Christianity spread over Asia and eventually captured Rome. From there the faith has spread world wide. Even today in Africa and Latin American countries, it continues a miraculous growth. In many places where the technological revolution has not fully captured the minds of the people, healings and miracles continue to be performed in His name.

The great theological breakthrough and the heart of the Gospel is that the *Messiah* must suffer, die, and rise again. By this mighty act of God, the world has been set on a path toward *conversion* to the *kingdom* without violating the free will given to man by God in the beginning. The sin of disobedience, pride, and egotism inherent in human nature was forgiven. The *Messiah* coming in humility and servant-hood and dying for *our* sins touches the most hardened heart, changing it from a heart of stone to a heart of flesh. The risen Lord fulfills the prophecy concerning the *Messiah* sitting on the throne of David forever. This would obviously be impossible for a mere human being. The resurrection indicates the final victory of God and gives mankind the hope of eternal life.

The covenant relationship between Israel and God which had played such an important role in "salvation history" found its final meaning in the coming, dying, and resurrection of Jesus Christ. He ushered in the *new covenant* prophesied by Jeremiah. Because of sin, man could not obey the Law. Jesus, the Son of God, shed his blood upon the cross and died for *our* sins, thereby washing away our sins, giving us a new relationship with God and writing God's laws upon our hearts. Jesus did for us what we could never do for ourselves.   Each time we celebrate the Holy Communion, we partake of the body and blood of Christ, remembering His death as the sacrifice for our sins and receiving His promises of redemption and eternal life in our new universally offered covenant with God.

From a personal point of view, Christianity holds the theological and practical answers to man's deepest questions. Who am I? Why am I here? What is my destiny? Where does my help come from in time of trouble? What lies beyond the grave? We find serenity and rest in the Savior especially when life gets hectic and difficult and when anxieties overwhelm us. And we remember that He said, "Come to me, all who labor and are heavy laden, and I will give you rest. Take my yoke upon you, and learn from me; for I am gentle and lowly in heart, and you will find rest for your souls, for my yoke is easy, and my burden is light."[156]

Regarding our final destiny, Jesus promised, "The sheep that are My own hear and are listening to My voice; and I know them, and they follow Me. And I give them eternal life, and they shall never lose it or perish throughout the ages. [To all eternity they shall never by any means be destroyed.] And no one is able to snatch them out of My hand."[157]

It is true that Jesus accomplished what no man had been able to do since the very beginning. In three years He taught us about the Father, the abundant life, and the *kingdom* of God. In one day He took away the sin of the world. In three days He defeated man's oldest enemy, death. And He is forever vindicated by His Father, Who blesses us with the continuous presence of His blessed Holy Spirit.

The real energy and life changing flame of the Gospel is found only in a Scripture-centered, orthodox faith. It is a beam of light which changes a life-taker into a life-giver, a villain into a saint, a

---

[156] Matt. 11:28-30 RSV.
[157] John 10: 27, 28 AB.

criminal into a born-again Christian. Deviations or revisionist movements lose the vitality and life giving force of the pure Gospel. God grant that I should stay within that wonderful beam of light which emanates from the Father through the Son by the power of the Holy Spirit. The Scripture itself is our best guide for keeping us in that light.

Revisionists get much publicity because of their novelty and presumed new intellectual thought. Their ideas make interesting TV and parlor talk, but rarely if ever change lives or heal people. Concerning our final destiny, they are perched in never-never land. And whereas the Scripture is quite clear and firm concerning the future, the revisionist is vague and generally agnostic.

Unfortunately during this present period, some Christians and most secularists have relegated Christianity to a ritualistic Sunday event. They have lost the excitement of God's saving grace, marginalized the faith, and forgotten or dismissed the revolutionary teaching, promises, and nature of the life of Jesus. Part of the purpose of this book is to attempt to refocus attention on real Christianity, to "expose" it again as the ultimate life and death choice and the most important issue facing every human being.

We give thanks to you, O God, for the goodness and love which you have made known to us in creation; in the calling of Israel to be your people; in your Word spoken through the prophets; and above all in the Word made flesh, Jesus, your Son. For in these last days you sent him to be incarnate from the Virgin Mary, to be the Savior and Redeemer of the world. In him, you have delivered us from evil, and made us worthy to stand before you. In him, you have brought us out of error into truth, out of sin into righteousness, out of death into life. [158]

----

[158] *Book of Common Prayer,* 1979. p.368.

1. Describe how the record of history validates Jesus' role as the *Messiah*.
2. Explain the covenant prophesied by Jeremiah. How did Jesus usher in this new universal covenant?
3. Tell how Jesus' role as God's *Messiah* has affected your life.
4. What is the promise of Jesus concerning our final destiny?
5. Is there evidence of Jesus' redemption in our broken world?
6. What can we do to spread the Gospel and convince others that accepting Jesus is the most important decision any person will ever make?

Recommended reading: Jeremiah 31:31-35
Hebrews Chapter 9
Romans 5: 1-11
Romans 3:21-26
1 Corinthians 11:23-26
Ephesians Chapter 1, Chapter 2
Philippians 2:5-11
Colossians 1:9-29
1Peter 2:23-25
Hebrews 13:20,21

Thirteen

The Kingdom of Heaven is Like...

For many years I have picked up every book that speaks about heaven. In all those times I have never found anything that even begins to satisfy my curiosity and yearnings. And I suspect I never will. Therefore I have to remain content with what the Scripture teaches. In this book I have repeatedly stated that the *kingdom* will be *like* the beginning of creation before man disobeyed God and sought to set his own boundaries of good and evil—in other words like the Garden of Eden as first described in Genesis.

In Matthew's Gospel there are many passages in which Jesus says that the *kingdom* of heaven is like some things we are familiar with. "Jesus put before them another parable, saying, 'The *kingdom* of heaven is like a grain of mustard seed which a man took and sowed in his field; it is the smallest of all seeds, but when it has grown it is the greatest of shrubs and becomes a tree, so that the birds of the air come and make nests in its branches.' He told them another parable, 'The *kingdom* of heaven is like leaven which a woman took and hid in three measures of flour, till it was all leavened... The *kingdom* of heaven is like treasure hidden in a field, which a man found and covered up; then in his joy he goes and sells all that he has and buys that field. Again, the *kingdom* of heaven is like a merchant in search of fine pearls, who on finding one pearl of great value, went and sold all that he had and bought it. And again, the *kingdom* of heaven is like a net which was thrown into the sea and gathered fish of every kind; when it was full, men drew it ashore and sat down and sorted the good into vessels but threw away the bad. So it will be at the close of the age.' "[159]

Isaiah describes a time when a shoot out of the stock of Jesse (David's father) shall reign on the earth. The Spirit of the Lord will rest upon Him. He shall have wisdom and understanding, and shall rule with righteousness. He shall treat the meek, the poor, and downtrodden with fairness. The breath of His mouth shall slay the wicked. At that time the wolf will live with the lamb, the leopard with the kid and the calf with the lion and a young child will lead them. This is one of several dimensions of the *kingdom* and coincides with the rule of Christ after the *Second Coming*. It is *related* to the return of conditions existing in the Garden of Eden.

In the book of Revelation, another dimension follows the thousand year reign of Christ on earth referred to above. After that time, evil (Satan and his followers) is finally and completely dealt with, and the *kingdom* of God is pictured as merging with the new heaven and new earth. God will dwell with men on the new earth. There will be no sickness, death, or sorrow. The grand human experiment will be brought to maturity, and like the Garden of Eden, a perfect paradise will again prevail. "Then I saw a new heaven and a new earth; for the first heaven and the first earth had passed away, and the sea was no more. And I saw the holy city, new Jerusalem, coming down out of heaven from God, prepared as a bride adorned for her husband; and I heard a great

---

[159] Matt. 13:31-33, 44-49a RSV (my italics).

voice from the throne saying, 'Behold, the dwelling of God is with men. He will dwell with them, and they shall be his people, and God himself will be with them; he will wipe away every tear from their eyes, and death shall be no more, neither shall there be mourning nor crying nor pain any more, for the former things have passed away.' "[160]

But these two dimensions are in the future. What does the Scripture teach us about the present? From the beginning of His ministry Jesus stated many times that the *kingdom* of heaven was near or at hand. When some great truth was taught or when some healing took place, Jesus stated that the *kingdom* of God had come *close*. It follows that the *kingdom* is a place of healing or of perpetual good health closely related to the "good news." The *kingdom* is consequently closely identified with Jesus, Himself, and He brought the *kingdom* to earth with its signs being healing, raising the dead, and other miracles. Driving out demons is an indication that the *kingdom* is overcoming the agents of the devil. Jesus said, "...If I drive out the demons by the finger of God, then the *kingdom* of God has [already] come upon you."[161]

Thus the *kingdom* has many dimensions, all of which share the same attributes and meanings. The *kingdom* as a movement or realm invaded earth at the appearance of Jesus, but it does not take complete hold. He is rejected by the Jewish nation, but the invasion is not blotted out. In fact, it grows as the church of Jesus Christ until it attains a prominent place in the world, but does not completely take it. Therefore the prayer is: *Thy kingdom come.* John's expression is that the darkness has not overcome it. Jesus says that the gates of hell will not prevail against it (the church).

---

[160] Revelation 21:1-4 RSV.
[161] Luke 11: 20 AB.

The signs of the invading *kingdom* are also closely related to the ethics of the prophets and of Jesus. No one can enter the *kingdom* who practices wicked deeds. Jesus said, "For I tell you, unless your righteousness (your uprightness and your right standing with God) is more than that of the Scribes and Pharisees, you will never enter the kingdom of heaven."[162] Jesus had accused the Pharisees of being hypocrites— observing the form of the Law but neglecting its substance of justice, mercy, and the love of God. Paul points out this principle very clearly when he actually makes a list of persons who cannot enter the *kingdom*. They include those who practice immorality, licentiousness, idolatry, sorcery, strife, jealousy, selfishness, envy and drunkenness.[163] The book of Revelation also makes this point quite clear, the list including the immoral, murderers, idolaters and those who deal in falsehood, deception and cheating. Jesus follows this line of thinking in parables concerning the *kingdom*.[164]

Jesus taught that the *kingdom* can be experienced on earth in the lives of the redeemed. Thus the expression, "...the kingdom of God is within you [in your hearts] and among you [surrounding you]."[165] This is another manifestation of *kingdom* invasion. We can manifest the *kingdom* in our lives and see it manifested in those around us—healings of body and spirit, experiences of the love Jesus proclaimed. So we can have a taste of the *kingdom* right here on earth.

In the Gospel of John the phrase, *kingdom* of God, is used in only two instances. In the first, Jesus states to Nicodemus that one must be *born again* in order to experience the *kingdom* of God. Then before Pilate, Jesus says, "My kingdom (kingship, royal

---

[162] Matt. 5: 20 AB.
[163] Based on Gal. 5: 19.
[164] See: Matt. 13: 24 ff, Matt. 13:47ff, Matt. 18: 23ff, Matt. 20: 1ff, Matt. 22:2ff, Matt. 25:1ff.
[165] Luke 17: 21b AB.

power) belongs not to this world. If my kingdom were of this world, My followers would have been fighting to keep me from being handed over to the Jews. But as it is, My kingdom is not here (this world); [it has no such origin or source]."[166] This implies clearly that the *kingdom* is a place, but not of this world.

In the Gospel of Luke, Jesus, in speaking to his Apostles, says, "And you are those who have remained [throughout] *and* persevered with Me in My trials; and as My Father has appointed a kingdom *and* conferred it on Me, so do I confer on you [the privilege and decree], that you may eat and drink at My table in My kingdom and sit on thrones, judging the twelve tribes of Israel."[167]

Jesus clearly taught that the *kingdom* is an actual place where repentant believers will go after life in this world. In John 14:1-3, Jesus tells his Apostles not to be troubled, but believe in God and believe also in Him. He then says that in His Father's house are many dwelling places and that He goes to prepare a place for them so that they may be with Him. It's the same place where Jesus went after the resurrection and ascension, to be at the right hand of God the Father. In the Gospel of Luke, Jesus tells the believing thief on the cross, "This day you will be with Me in Paradise." Obviously, a place is indicated and the thief's change of heart earns him an entrance to that place where Jesus will be going. Earlier in Luke, Jesus tells the apostles, "Do not be afraid, little flock, for it is your Father's good pleasure to give you the *kingdom*."[168]

It is a place of infinite beauty and thrilling life, where sorrow and death are no more. It is the place from which Jesus and His heavenly hosts will again invade earth at the *Second Coming* at the end of the age. It is a place where believers will feast at table with

---

[166] John 18: 36 AB.
[167] Luke 22:28, 29, 30 AB.
[168] Luke 12:32 NRSV (my italics).

Jesus. It is a place where one constantly experiences the presence of God and joyfully worships Him.

The *kingdom* is not restricted to any race or nation. Jesus said, "And [people] will come from east and west, and from north and south, and sit down (feast at table) in the kingdom of God."[169]

After Jesus assured the Apostles about the *kingdom*, Thomas, who had a way of asking difficult questions, asks how they will know the way to get there. There follows this memorable and remarkable reply, "I am the way and the truth and the life; no one comes to the Father, but by Me."[170] The closest we can come to finding the *kingdom* is just to follow Jesus, accept Him, trust in Him and He will lead us there.

----

1. Name three familiar things Jesus says the kingdom of God is like.
2. Describe the Revelation picture of the kingdom of God.
3. What did Jesus mean when He stated that the *kingdom* of heaven had come close?
4. According to the Gospel of John, what did Jesus say was required before a person could enter the *kingdom* of God? Explain fully.
5. Describe at least two instances where Jesus referred to the *kingdom* of God as an actual place to be experienced by the faithful after life in this world.
6. Describe your own concept of the *kingdom* of heaven and your own means of getting there.

Recommended reading: Matthew 13:24-50

---

[169] Luke 13:29 AB. See also Rev. 7:9.
[170] John 14:6 RSV.

Mark 1:9-15
Luke 13:18-30
John 3:1-15
John 14:1-6
Galatians 5:16-24
Hebrews 11:8-10, 13-16
Revelation 21:1-7

Fourteen

Eternal Life

To be a Christian is to have the very highest regard for human life. It even goes so far as to have a respect for all life and to refrain from taking the life of animals unless it serves a useful human need or purpose. That's why many Christians are in the pro-life column instead of the pro-choice one. And that's why late term abortions are so adamantly opposed by Christians.

It is not a far step to understand then that most Christians believe in the promises of God set forth by Jesus Christ. These promises about eternal life are believed by those who have the highest regard for human life and firmly believe that God values life even more than we do. It is completely rational to expect that God would grant eternal life to those who have accepted Jesus, his Son, and have tried to carry out His will. Too much has been invested in every such life for it to simply end in death.

While the Gospel of John mentions the *kingdom* of God only twice,[171] the theme of eternal life is dealt with more times than in the synoptics, Matthew, Mark, and Luke. The two topics are closely related. Those who enter the *kingdom* will be blessed with eternal life. Living in the *kingdom* will mean enjoying the presence of God forever— worshiping Him, serving Him and taking part in a life of unbelievable beauty and accomplishing thrilling missions which He will give us. So in the Gospel of John, eternal life becomes almost synonymous with the *kingdom*. We can therefore become better acquainted with the *kingdom* by examining the term *eternal life* in John.

Life is in God the Father and also in Jesus Christ, His Son. "For even as the Father has life in Himself and is self-existent, so He has given to the Son to have life in Himself *and* be self-existent. And He has given Him authority *and* granted Him power to execute (exercise, practice) judgment…"[172] Life or eternal life is given to humans by the Son according to the will of the Father. That is why the statement by Jesus that no one can come to the Father but by Him (Jesus) is truly and essentially a Gospel statement.

The most familiar passage in John follows this same principle: "For God so greatly loved and dearly prized the world that He [even] gave up His only begotten (unique) Son, so that whoever believes in (trusts in, clings to, relies on) Him shall not perish (come to destruction, be lost) but have eternal (everlasting) life.[173] Eternal life is the gift of God to those who accept His Son as Master and Savior of their lives. And that, of course, implies in the strongest way the acceptance of Jesus' teachings and commandments, striving to walk in His way. Jesus said, "…but strive *and* work *and* produce rather for the [lasting] food which endures [continually] into life eternal; the Son of Man will give

---

[171] John 3:3,5; 18:36.
[172] John 5:26, 27a AB.
[173] John 3:16 AB.

(furnish) you that, for God the Father has authorized and certified Him and put His seal of endorsement upon Him."[174]

And again to reinforce these statements, Jesus said, "For the Bread of God is He Who comes down out of heaven and gives *life* to the world."[175] When Jesus made the statement that those who eat his flesh and drink his blood have eternal life, many of the disciples could not comprehend his meaning and some even turned away and left.[176] Jesus asked the Twelve, "Will you also go away? [And do you too desire to leave me?] Simon Peter answered, "Lord to whom shall we go? You have the words [message] of eternal life. And we have learned to believe *and* trust, and [more] we have come to know [surely] that you are *the Holy One of God*, the Christ (the Anointed One), the Son of the living God."[177] *When faced with hard choices in today's world, will we too turn away?*

The gift of eternal life is not some vague, future promise as John makes clear in many passages. For example, "I assure you, most solemnly I tell you, he who believes in Me [who adheres to, trusts in, relies on, and has faith in Me] has (now possesses) eternal life."[178]

---

[174] John 6:27b AB.

[175] John 6:33 AB (my italics).

[176] Jesus was making one of His hard sayings, meaning that his followers must have His life within them. Jewish law and tradition prevented them from eating or drinking blood, so the saying was extremely hard for those who observed this prohibition. The Holy Communion Service following the instruction of Jesus at the last supper is the church's way of bringing to present mind or remembrance this admonition.

[177] John 6:67b, 68,69 AB.

[178] John 6:47 AB This statement is closely related to another by Jesus in John 17:3, "And this is eternal life: [it means] to know (to perceive, recognize, become acquainted with, and understand) You, the only true and real God and (likewise) to know Him, Jesus [as the] Christ (the Anointed One, the Messiah) Whom You have sent." (same version)

But Jesus not only made these stunning promises of God, He demonstrated them. He showed that He indeed has *life* in himself in His resurrection from the dead. Even before His death and resurrection, He proclaimed, "For this reason the Father loves me, because I lay down my life, that I may take it up again. No one takes it from me, but I lay it down of my own accord. I have power to lay it down, and I have power to take it up again; this charge I have received from my Father."[179]   Before He raised Lazarus from the dead, He told Martha, "I am the resurrection and the life; he who believes in me, though he die, yet shall he live, and whoever lives and believes in me shall never die."[180]

I believe that according to Genesis, eternal life was part of God's plan for creation before mankind exercised its God-given freedom, disobeyed and rebelled against the Creator.[181]   I believe that it is in God's plan to restore that paradise by reconciling mankind to Himself. He sent Jesus to bring this process to fruition by teaching and demonstrating His great love for his creation, and He sent His Holy Spirit to empower us and guarantee our inheritance in His *kingdom*. But we have to exercise *our freedom by choosing* to accept His Son. The "prize," as Paul puts it, is the gift of eternal life in the *kingdom* of God.

Dear People of God: Our heavenly Father sent his Son into the world, not to condemn the world, but that the world through him might be saved; that all who believe in him might be delivered from the power of sin and death, and become heirs with him of everlasting life.[182]

----

[179] John 10:17, 18 RSV.

[180] John 11: 25 b, 26 a, RSV.

[181] See Gen. 1: 26, 27: Gen. 2: 16, 17 and Rom 5: 12-18.

[182] *The Book of Common Prayer*, 1979 p. 277.

1. Explain the relationship between the imperfect form of the Hebrew verb, *to be* (YHWH) and the term, *eternal life*. How do these expressions relate to the *kingdom* of God?
2. What did Jesus mean by saying that a person must eat His flesh and drink His blood in order to have eternal life?
3. Name at least two promises of God made through Jesus Christ about eternal life.
4. What are the reasons the Holy Communion service is so important to the church?
5. Describe your own concept of eternal life.

Recommended reading: Job 19:25-27a
John 10:1-18
John 6: 25-69
John 14:1-6
John 5:19-29
John 12: 47-50
Mark 14:22-24
Philippians 3:4b-21
Romans 6:20-23, Romans 8:1-14
1 Corinthians Chapter 15
2 Corinthians 4:13- Chapter 5:5
1 Thessalonians 4:13- Chapter 5:11
1 Peter 1:3-5
2 Peter 1:3-11

Fifteen

Waiting...The Periods In-Between

One problem with people of every historical period is discerning the hand of God actively working in the world. In the present period between the *First Coming* of Christ and the *Second Coming*, Christians are hungry to see evidence of the mighty God. Perhaps that is the reason the charismatic renewal of the 1960's, 70's and 80's drew so much interest and attention. This special Baptism of the Holy Spirit was a supernatural move of God. The Spirit's work in healings, conversions, deliverances, prophecies, and tongues showed that God is indeed active in His creation.

Faith and patience are important attributes during these periods. Daily Bible reading, prayer, and meditation are essential to keeping a healthy spiritual life. Association with other Christians in worship and in small groups adds depth to our encounters with God.

Skepticism concerning God's willingness or ability to act in human affairs belies the Jewish and Christian concepts of the immanent Creator, Who has an abiding and ever present interest in His creation. There are simply things which mankind alone cannot accomplish. The active participation of the Creator is necessary if God's plan and purpose are to be carried out. Without God the Law never would have been written. Sin could not have been taken away without the direct intervention of God. The Gospel could never have been proclaimed to the world without the power of the Holy Spirit. Conversions, spiritual healings, and deliverances would not occur without great faith exercised in the saving grace of God's Son.

Every age has its skeptics both in and out of the church. Many have been influenced by scientific rationalism, which has deep roots in the culture of Western nations. Some Christian denominations maintain that miracles or supernatural acts of God ceased after the period of the Apostles or when the church gained a strong foothold. I find no scriptural evidence to support such a belief.

If we think today that our period of waiting is too burdensome, a comparison with other periods will raise our spirits. Suppose we were living in the period after the prophets of Israel and before the *First Coming* of Christ. Our major consolation might be the words of the prophets who proclaimed the *future coming of the Messiah*. But we would have to wait many generations, about 400 years before that prophecy was actually fulfilled. The Jews were slaves of the Egyptians for about 400 years before Moses was called by God to free them. The time lapse between the destruction of Jerusalem and the re-establishment of Israel as a nation lasted from 70 A.D. until 1948 A.D. God's time is not our time and the movement of His plan seems to progress very slowly according to human standards, which is basically measured in terms of a normal life span.

One problem with our impatience is an actual misconception of God's plan. For instance, if we are waiting for *all* mankind to become converted to Christ, we are probably waiting in vain. In the teachings of Jesus including the Olivet Discourse (Matthew

24) there is no suggestion that all will be converted or saved. The skeptics, the atheists, and those who continually plan evil will always be with us, even though the Gospel will be preached in all the world. God-given freedom always allows us to make our own choices and some will continue to eat the wrong "apple."

We must remember, however, that it is still our calling (by Christ, Himself) to *try* to bring all people into His *kingdom*. It is our responsibility to do this especially in the way God has provided for us, using the talents He has given us and the gifts of the Holy Spirit. There is one thing we can count on concerning the *Second Coming*. It will come at a time when it is totally unexpected. Jesus said, "As were the days of Noah, so will be the coming of the Son of Man. For just as in those days before the flood they were eating and drinking, [men] marrying and [women] being given in marriage, until the [very] day when Noah went into the ark. And they did not know *or* understand until the flood came and swept them all away—so will be the coming of the Son of Man."[183]

In spite of the trials and difficulties we all face, we must be thankfully aware of the special privileges God has given us in this age. We are the age which has heard the good news, the Gospel! Jesus said, "Truly, I say to you, many prophets and righteous men longed to see what you see, and did not see it, and to hear what you hear, and did not hear it."[184]

We can elect to accept Jesus as Lord and Savior and receive the Holy Spirit. We can constantly study the Word of God in Holy Scripture, and we can use the gifts which have been given us. We can see that some prophecies have already been fulfilled, that miracles are still happening, and that God's purpose is slowly but definitely moving forward. We can look expectantly for the *Second Coming* and the *kingdom* of God.

---

[183] Matt. 24:37-39 AB.
[184] Matt. 13: 17 RSV.

We are living in an age blessed by the Son of Man. There is no longer a barrier between us and God, so we can confess directly to the Creator, pleading the blood of Jesus shed for our sins on the cross. We can repent, receive His forgiveness, and rely on His promises made to us by His Christ. With such blessings, how can we restrain from thanking and glorifying God every day? And how can we not be excited about our future made blessed and secure by Jesus the Christ? "For God so loved the world that He gave His only Son, that whoever believes in him should not perish but have eternal life."[185]

O rest in the Lord, wait patiently for Him,
and He shall give thee thy heart's desires;
O rest in the Lord, wait patiently for Him,
and He shall give thee thy heart's desires.
Commit thy way unto Him, and trust in Him,
and fret not thyself because of evil doers.
O rest in the Lord, wait patiently for Him,
and He shall give thee thy heart's desires.[186]

----

1. Which period of history would have been the most difficult to live in?
2. Describe how you perceive the hand of God working in the world today.
3. Name at least three advantages the present age has in regard to human destiny and the meaning of life.
4. What gifts can you use to bring others into the *kingdom* of God?

---

[185] John 3:16 RSV.

[186] Adapted from an oratorio, *Elijah* by Felix Mendelssohn (1809-1847), No. 31, "O Rest in the Lord." Words were probably based on Psalm 37.

Recommended reading: 2 Peter Chapter 3
Matthew 26:26-29
Matthew 28:16-20
1 Corinthians 1:4-9
1 Corinthians 1:20-Chapter 2:16
Hebrews 11:1- Chapter 12:3
Ephesians 4:1-Chapter 5:20
Philippians 4:4-7

Sixteen

The Second Coming of Christ

After the resurrection, Jesus presented Himself to the apostles for forty days, speaking of the *kingdom* of God. He also charged them not to depart from Jerusalem until they had been baptized by the Holy Spirit to receive power. On the last day of His appearing, He and the apostles were gathered together on the Mount of Olives. The apostles asked Him again when He would restore the kingdom to Israel, showing that they still did not fully comprehend the meaning of His coming to earth. His answer was "... you shall receive power when the Holy Spirit has come upon you; and you shall be my witnesses in Jerusalem and in all Judea and Samaria and to the end of the earth."[187]

After saying this, He was taken up in a cloud. The apostles were still gazing up into the sky when two men in white robes stood by them and said, "Men of Galilee, why do you stand looking into heaven? This Jesus, who was taken up from you into

---

[187] Acts 1: 8b RSV.

heaven, *will come in the same way as you saw him go into heaven.*" [188] The book of Acts thereby witnesses to the *Second Coming* of the Lord.

Earlier, Jesus himself had clearly indicated that He would come again. That scene was also the Mount of Olives when Jesus disclosed some of the signs of the last days. He said, "And because wickedness is multiplied, most men's love will grow cold. But he who endures to the end will be saved...For as the lightning comes from the east and shines as far as the west, so will be the coming of the Son of man...."[189] He told them that after the tribulation[190] the sun would be darkened, the moon would lose its light and stars would fall from heaven. Then the sign of the Son of Man would appear in the heavens and all the tribes of the earth would mourn,[191] for they will see the Son of Man coming on the clouds of heaven with great power and glory. He would then send His angels to gather His elect from one end of the heaven to the other.

The *Second Coming* of Christ coincides with many pictures of the *Messiah* found in the prophets of Israel.[192] For example, Jeremiah prophesied:

> "Behold, *the* days are coming," declares the Lord,
> "When I will raise up for David a righteous Branch;
> And He will reign as king and act wisely

---

[188] Acts 1: 11 RSV (my italics).

[189] Matt. 24: 27 RSV.

[190] Jesus says of the tribulation, "For then there will be great tribulation such as has not been from the beginning of the world until now, no, and never will be. And if those days had not been shortened, no human being would be saved." Matt. 24:21,22a RSV. The prophets all speak of the tribulation in much the same way.

[191] The Jews would mourn because they previously had rejected Christ. The Gentiles would mourn because they had become so entrapped by the wealth and glamour of the world that they had forgotten or neglected Christ.

[192] Again, Old Testament prophecy is bifocal, some fulfillment in the first coming of Jesus, the rest in the second coming.

And do justice and righteousness in the land.
In His days Judah will be saved,
And Israel will dwell securely;
And this is His name by which He will be called,
'The Lord our righteousness.' [193]

Similar passages are found in Ezekiel, Daniel, and the first portion of Isaiah.[194] All these passages can be related back to the prophecy about the kingdom of David (Israel's ideal king), when Nathan prophesied to David that his kingdom would be made sure forever, his throne established forever. The prophecy then comes closer with the coming of Jesus, whose earthly parents were both of the linage of David. The fulfillment draws near when Jesus returns to earth to reign for a thousand years on the throne of David in the age before eternity.[195] The resurrected Lord, being greater than a mortal king, can do this.

The letters of Peter and Paul can shed further light on the *Second Coming.* Peter's second letter addresses the impatience of skeptics. "...scoffers will come in the last days with scoffing, following their own passions and saying, 'Where is the promise of his coming? For ever since the fathers fell asleep, all things have continued as they were from the beginning of creation.' "[196] Peter says that such people ignore the fact that the heavens and earth were created by the Word of God and that a thousand years is as one day with the Lord. He further states that one reason the *Second Coming* has been delayed is to give all people a chance to repent, and that the day of His coming will be like a thief, sudden and unexpected.

Paul describes the Lord's coming as follows: "For the Lord himself will descend from heaven with a cry of command, with

---

[193] Jeremiah 23: 5 , 6 NASB.
[194] Ezekiel 34: 23, 24; 37: 24 Dan. 7: 13, 14 Isaiah 9: 6.7; 11: 1-10.
[195] Rev. 20.
[196] 2 Peter 3:3b, 4 RSV.

the archangel's call, and with the sound of the trumpet of God. And the dead in Christ will rise first, then we who are alive, who are left, shall be caught up together with them in the clouds to meet the Lord in the air; and so we shall always be with the Lord."[197] In Revelation, a letter from Christ to the church in Philadelphia (an ancient city in Asia) reads, "...Because you have kept my word of patient endurance, I will keep you from the hour of trial which is coming on the whole world...." [198] Taking these two passages together, some Christians believe that Christ will return to earth to call the true and faithful church into heaven before the harsh trials of the tribulation begin. The best selling "Left Behind" series of novels is based on this premise.

Paul further describes the Lord's coming: "When Christ who is our life appears, then you also will appear with him in glory."[199] And in Philippians Paul says, "But our commonwealth is in heaven, and from it we await a Savior, the Lord Jesus Christ, who *will change our lowly body to be like his glorious body, by the power which enables him even to subject all things to himself.*"[200] And in 2 Thessalonians, "...God deems it just to repay with affliction those who afflict you, and to grant rest with us to you who are afflicted, when the Lord Jesus is revealed from heaven with his mighty angels in flaming fire, inflicting vengeance upon those who do not know God and upon those who do not obey the gospel of our Lord Jesus."[201]

The most vivid descriptions of the *Second Coming* are found in Revelation. The first is very similar to what Jesus describes in the Olivet Discourse. "Behold, he is coming with the clouds, and every eye will see him, every one who pierced him; and all tribes of the earth will wail on account of him."[202] The second is full of

---

[197] 1 Thess. 4:16, 17 RSV.
[198] Rev. 3: 10 RSV.
[199] Col. 3: 4 RSV.
[200] Phil. 3: 20, 21 RSV. (my italics)
[201] 2 Thess. 1:6-8 RSV.
[202] Rev. 1: 7 RSV.

the rich imagery of Revelation: "Then I saw heaven opened, and behold, a white horse. He who sat upon it is called Faithful and True, and in righteousness he judges and makes war. His eyes are like a flame of fire, and on his head are many diadems; and he has a name inscribed which no one knows but himself. He is clad in a robe dipped in blood, and the name by which he is called is The Word of God. And the armies of heaven, arrayed in fine linen, white and pure, followed him on white horses."[203]

It is clear from all these passages that Scripture teaches us that Christ will come again. According to Revelation, He will come the second time as the Lion of Judah, far different from the first coming as the Lamb of God. The time of the *Second Coming* is known only by God the Father, but it will signal the maturity of the human experiment, the end of the age. Scripture warns us to be alert and watchful, for the *Second Coming* will be unexpected and sudden and we don't want to be unprepared with our focus on the things of this world.

Come, Thou long expected Jesus,
Born to set Thy people free;
From our fears and sins release us;
Let us find our rest in Thee.

Israel's strength and consolation,
Hope of all the earth Thou art;
Dear desire of every nation,
Joy of every longing heart.

Born Thy people to deliver,
Born a child and yet a king,
Born to reign in us forever,
Now Thy gracious kingdom bring.[204]

---

[203] Rev. 19: 11-14 RSV.
[204] First portion of a hymn written by Charles Wesley (1707-1788).

----

1. Describe the difference between the first coming and the *Second Coming* of Jesus. Name the major purpose of each coming. What titles describe Jesus in the first coming and the *Second Coming*?
2. What most important prophecy was made to David concerning the kingdom? Name the prophet.
3. What are some of the signs preceding the *Second Coming* according to Jesus?
4. How can we be prepared for the *Second Coming*?

Recommended reading: Acts 1:1-14
                                  2 Samuel 7:4-17
                                  Isaiah 11:1-5
                                  Matthew Chapter 24

Seventeen

Revelation and End Times

The Bible needed a book picturing the conclusion of the human experiment in its promising beginning, its fallen futility, its horrendous history, and its final spectacular beauty. The church fathers discerned the divine authority of the book written by John, the beloved disciple of Jesus. No one was better equipped to do such an awesome job than the disciple who had been so close to our Lord and who had lived much longer than the others and who was guided by the Holy Spirit. No one was as familiar with the writings of the prophets and the entire Old Testament. No one knew our Lord any better.

I do not believe that Revelation has been taught or fully accepted in the church like the other books of the Bible. I further believe that this is partly due to the vivid imagery which John employs, the perception that the understanding is difficult, and the pastoral concern over many fundamentalist interpretations. John tells the story as a series of visions he experienced when "in the Spirit." There is the marvelous picture of God's throne in heaven:

"At once I was in the Spirit, and lo, a throne stood in heaven, with one seated on the throne! And he who sat there appeared like jasper and carnelian, and round the throne was a rainbow that looked like an emerald. Round the throne were twenty-four thrones, and seated on the thrones were   twenty-four elders, clad in white garments, with golden crowns upon their heads. From the throne issue flashes of lightning and voices and peals of thunder, and before the throne burn seven torches of fire, which are the seven spirits of God; and before the throne there is as it were a sea of glass, like crystal."[205]

The well known hymn, *Holy, Holy, Holy*, second verse, is derived from Revelation. "Holy, Holy, Holy, all the saints adore thee, casting down their golden crowns before the glassy sea."[206]

There is also a visionary picture of Jesus. A scroll with seven seals is seen in the hand of God, but no one in heaven or earth is worthy to open the scroll until Jesus, the Lion of Judah and the root of David, comes forth appearing as a Lamb who had been slain. He alone is worthy to open the scroll because by his blood He did ransom people for God from every tribe, tongue, people, and nation to make them a *kingdom* and priests to God.[207]

But it is the *Second Coming* of Christ and the establishment of the *kingdom* of God that provide the link to our story. At earth's darkest hour when Satan seems to have the upper hand, the heavens (clouds) open and Jesus comes forth on a white horse with the armies of heaven.[208] At this *Second Coming* He is the Lion of Judah ready to do battle with the forces of Satan.

---

[205] Rev. 4: 2-6a RSV.
[206] Written by Reginald Heber (1783-1826).
[207] Based on Rev. 5:9,10 (my italics).
[208] Rev. 19:11,14.

When Jesus has won the battle of Armageddon, He establishes His *kingdom* for a thousand years on the earth.[209] This *kingdom* partially fulfills the prophecy concerning the throne of David being established forever.

The prophecy is completed when after the thousand year rule of Christ, another battle takes place ending Satan's evil role forever, and God brings forth a new heaven (sky) and a new earth. God and the Lamb will dwell there in eternity with all faithful people, living and resurrected in a joyful and everlasting *kingdom*.[210]

Through this prophetic and apocalyptic series of visions, John writes a grand conclusion to the greatest book ever written. In studying and teaching Revelation, I found that the book is not nearly as difficult as I had been led to believe. Anyone generally familiar with the Old and New Testament will perceive and understand most of the images and the drama. For instance, the book of Daniel makes a perfect overlay for Revelation with the time sequences fitting perfectly.

The truths presented in Revelation are well within my core Christian beliefs. I highly recommend the study of Revelation (and Daniel) for a complete understanding of the conclusion of the Bible story and as a preparation for end times should they occur in our lifetime.

And I heard a loud voice from the throne saying,
> *"See, the home of God is among mortals.*
> *He will dwell with them as their God;*
> *They will be his peoples,*
> *And God himself will be with them;*
> *He will wipe every tear from their eyes.*

---

[209] Based on Rev. 20:4,5.
[210] Based on Rev. 21.

Death will be no more;
Mourning and crying and pain will be no more,
For the first things have passed away." [211]

What were the Apostle John's qualifications for writing the conclusion of the Bible?

1. Describe John's vision of Jesus' *Second Coming*.
2. What did John and Daniel have in common?
3. Some Christians think Revelation is largely symbolic. Others take it more literally. Describe your own thoughts.
4. Describe your own vision of what living in eternity with God and the Lamb will be like.

Recommended reading: Revelation: Chapter 5
                    Revelation 7:9-17
                    Revelation 19:4-21
                    Revelation 21:1-8
                    Daniel 7:19-28 ?
                    Daniel 12:1-4
                    Hebrews 12:18-29

---

[211] Rev. 21:3,4 NRSV with all margin words capitalized.

Epilogue—The Garden Regained

Satan and all his wicked forces have been defeated. Evil doers and enemies of God and His Christ have been judged and expelled. The truly repentant, the redeemed, and all those who have kept the faith, living and resurrected, have been brought together in God's new *kingdom*. The new creation has many similarities to the initial creation, the Garden where God first brought forth the human race. Nature is under control. There is no sickness or death. God provides ample fruit trees and harvests and heals all differences between nations. Wild animals put away their hostility and dwell together with tame animals. The bodies of the faithful will be like that of the risen Christ, imperishable and made to last forever. And most important of all, God and the Lamb will dwell with mankind. This is the Biblical picture of eternity.

I don't for one minute believe that this experience will be without any work or challenge.[212] God will provide that also and use His people to accomplish His objectives, whatever they might be. His people, having gone through the trials, persecutions, and hard experiences of unredeemed earth, are fully capable of

---

[212] Gen. 2:15.

handling His assignments and more than willing to joyfully worship and thankfully obey their Creator.

So we have come almost full circle from the initial Creation in all its beauty, splendor and perfection through the long age of man's egotism, rebellion and disobedience to the threshold of the *kingdom* of God. The signs of the times are very visible. Israel, after almost 2000 years of being dispersed, is again a nation in its original homeland. Knowledge has expanded geometrically through the computer and information highway. There is a large increase in lawlessness—a worldwide insurrection against the civilized world and against the Law. The Gospel is being preached in all the world by the true church of Jesus Christ. All of these are Biblical signs of the end times.[213] But arriving at the threshold does not mean we are ready to enter the paradise of God. As we have understood, God's time is not man's time. We could dally on the threshold for ten or a hundred years or we could see the culmination of God's plan very soon.

Regardless of the time question, the way to the *kingdom* has been made clear to us by the *Christ*, himself. He alone is God's Good Shepherd, who is known by His followers. He alone is the Way to the *kingdom* of God, and He alone is the Door by which we must enter. Receiving the *Christ* is the way to the *kingdom*. Glory be to God for His unfathomable mercy, grace, and goodness. And eternal thanks be to God for sending us the most precious gift of all—His blessed Son, our Savior, our Redeemer and our Righteousness.

---

[213] See Israel gathered: Amos 9:14,15, Micah 4:6,7, Ezekiel 39:25-29 and other prophets.
Knowledge expanded: Daniel 12:4. Lawlessness increased: Matthew 24:12.
Gospel preached to all the world: Matt. 24:14.

THEREFORE,   SINCE   these [great] promises are ours, beloved, let us cleanse ourselves from everything that contaminates *and* defiles body and spirit, and bring [our] consecration to completeness in the [reverential] fear of God.[214]

And may the God of peace Himself sanctify you through and through; and may your spirit, soul and body be kept sound, complete, and blameless at the coming of our Lord, Jesus Christ, the Messiah.[215]

---

[214] 2 Cor. 7:1 AB
[215]Based on I Thess. 5:23 AB .

Bibliography

Butler, John G. 1993. *Abraham, The Father of the Jews.* Clinton, Iowa.

De Haan, M.R. 1995. *Daniel the Prophet.* Grand Rapids, Michigan.

Hickey, Marilyn. 1997. *Psalms, Classic Library Edition.* Denver, Colorado.

Kidner, Derek. 1987. *The Message of Jeremiah.* Downers Grove, Illinois.

Motyer, J. Alec. 1999. *Isaiah.* Downers Grove, Illinois.

Spurgeon, Charles Haddon. (Updated by Roy H. Clarke) *The Treasury of David.* 1997.
Nashville, Tennessee.

Tidball, Derek. 2005. *The Message of Leviticus.* Downers Grove, Illinois.

Wood, Leon J. 1979. *The Prophets of Israel.* Grand Rapids, Michigan.

Webb, Barry G. 1996. *The Message of Isaiah.* Downers Grove, Illinois.

Webb, Barry G. 2003. *The Message of Zechariah.* Downers Grove, Illinois.

Holman Bible Dictionary. 1991. Nashville, Tennessee.

Harper's Bible Dictionary. 1952, 1954, 1955, 1956, 1958, 1959, 1961. New York,

Evanston, and London.
The Liberty Illustrated Bible Dictionary. 1986. Nashville, Camden, and New York.

The Holy Bible, Revised Standard Version (Cited RSV). 1946, 1952. Toronto, New
York, Edinburgh.

The Amplified Bible (cited AB). 1954, 1958, 1962, 1964, 1965, 1987. Grand Rapids,
Michigan.

New American Standard Bible (cited NASB). 1960, 1962, 1963,1968,1971,1973, 1975,
1977, 1995. Grand Rapids, Michigan.

The Holy Bible, New Revised Standard Version (cited NRSV). 1989. New York, New
York.

The Holy Bible, King James Version (cited KJV).

The Book of Common Prayer, 1979.

The Dead Sea Scrolls Bible, translated and with commentary by Martin Abegg, Jr., Peter Flint, and Eugene Ulrich. 1999. New York, New York.

Printed in the United States
68266LVS00001B/118-615